San Diego Padres 2019

A Baseball Companion

Edited by Patrick Dubuque, Aaron Gleeman and Bret Sayre

Baseball Prospectus

Craig Brown and Dave Pease, Consultant Editors
Rob McQuown and Harry Pavlidis, Statistics Editors

Copyright © 2019 by DIY Baseball, LLC.
All rights reserved

This book or any part thereof may not be reproduced or transmitted in any form or by any means, electronic or mechanical, including photocopying, recording, or by any information storage and retrieval system, without permission in writing from the publisher.

Limit of Liability/Disclaimer of Warranty: While the publisher and the author have used their best efforts in preparing this book, they make no representations or warranties with respect to the accuracy or completeness of the contents of this book and specifically disclaim any implied warranties of merchantability or fitness for a particular purpose. No warranty may be created or extended by sales representatives or written sales materials. The advice and strategies contained herein may not be suitable for your situation. You should consult with a professional where appropriate. Neither the publisher nor the author shall be liable for any loss of profit or any other commercial damages, including but not limited to special, incidental, consequential, or other damages.

Library of Congress Cataloging-in-Publication Data:
paperback
ISBN-13: 978-1-949332-52-0

Project Credits
Cover Design: Kathleen Dyson
Interior Design and Production: Jeff Pease, Dave Pease
Layout: Jeff Pease, Dave Pease

Baseball icon courtesy of Uberux, from https://www.shareicon.net/author/uberux

Ballpark diagram courtesy of Lou Spirito/THIRTY81 Project, https://thirty81project.com/

Manufactured in the United States of America
10 9 8 7 6 5 4 3 2 1

Table of Contents

Foreword v
    Rob Mains

Statistical Introduction vii

Part 1: Team Analysis

Table for Two: Previewing the 2019 San Diego Padres 3
    Sean Addis and Lance Brozdowski

Performance Graphs 9

2018 Team Performance 10

2019 Team Projections 11

Team Personnel 12

Petco Park Stats 13

Padres Team Analysis 15

Part 2: Player Analysis

Padres Player Analysis 20

Padres Prospects 103

Part 3: Featured Articles

The Hole in The Shift is Fixing Itself 119
    Russell Carleton

The State of the Quality Start 123
    Rob Mains

Heads-Up Hacking—The First Pitch 129
    Matthew Trueblood

A Hymn for the Index Stat 135
    Patrick Dubuque

Index of Names 139

Foreword

Rob Mains

Welcome to this companion of the 2019 San Diego Padres. We at Baseball Prospectus are excited to provide this analysis of the Padres.

Our website, Baseball Prospectus, is a leader in delivering high-quality commentary and data to baseball fans everywhere. To some, those words—commentary and data—appear mutually exclusive. There are people out there who believe that traditional analysis and advanced analytics must run on different paths. But the simplistic narrative of stats vs. traditionalists just isn't true. Every team's analytics department interacts with scouting, development, and major league operations with a common goal: Delivering a championship. New technologies, like radar tracking of pitch speeds and movement, enable talent evaluators to focus on qualitative aspects of pitching like mechanics and pitch sequencing. In-game strategies like infield shifts, based on batters' hit tendencies, help turn balls in play into outs. Hitters use information to adjust their swings to maximize run production.

All these numbers can seem, at best, intimidating, and at worst, counterproductive to the casual fan. Even as technology and analysis have embedded themselves deeply into the way teams run, it can often feel like statistics create a displacement between the viewer and the sport, breaking them out of the action. And yet every fan incorporates the numbers to some degree; stats like batting average and earned run average, so fundamental to how we talk about performance, are actually complicated formulas. They don't bother people because those formulas have become second nature, as easy to translate as the action on the field.

Along the way, new statistics have entered baseball's lexicon. You'll see some of them, like on-base percentage (which measures a batter's ability to get on base via walk, hit batter, or hit), OPS (on-base plus slugging), and average exit velocity (the speed of balls off a hitter's bat) on broadcasts. Others, like DRC+, might well be new to you. Some of them have been well-defined to the public, others haven't. That lack of context has created ambiguity. Fans know that a ball hit 100 mph is scorched, but does that mean extra bases? (Not if it's hit on the ground or high in the air it doesn't.)

For those who are amenable to them, the new statistics can increase the enjoyment and understanding of the game. They can help fans identify when a pitcher is tiring, when a stolen base or a bunt attempt makes sense (and, more often, when it doesn't), or how a team's lineup might be constructed. Websites like Baseball Prospectus add to that understanding by weaving metrics into the narrative of the game. That's the goal of this publication: to take some of the newer, more complicated statistics and make them as intuitive as the ones on the back of old baseball cards.

But you don't need to love analytics to love baseball. The fans at BP who worked together to write this guide are captivated first and foremost by the game itself. We're drawn to Aaron Judge's power, Francisco Lindor's glove, Billy Hamilton's speed and Patrick Corbin's slider and don't need numbers to tell us why they're so mesmerizing. The underlying statistics provide depth to the game that we all love.

We hope you'll find that this guide helps you better understand the Padres. Our analysts have studied the team's major league personnel and its minor league affiliates to identify their strengths and weaknesses, both the obvious ones and those that only a careful dissection of players' performances—yes, including the data—can reveal. You don't need us to tell you who was good and who wasn't in 2018, but our models and writers can help you project how each player is going to perform this year and beyond, and appreciate the greatness of each new game as it unfolds. As in the sport itself, the human and analytic components combine to generate a deeper overall understanding.

Think back to the first time you saw a baseball game on a high-definition TV. You'd grown familiar with how the game looked and felt on a picture tube. But new TV allowed you to see details that you'd never seen before. That's how advanced statistics work. The game itself is why you're here and why you're buying this. (And, for that matter, why we wrote it.) The statistical measures provide the sharper focus, the detail, the depth of knowledge that you didn't have before, generating an overall superior picture. Enjoy the view.

—Rob Mains is an author of Baseball Prospectus.

Statistical Introduction

Sports are, fundamentally, a blend of athletic endeavor and storytelling. Baseball, like any other sport, tells its stories in so many ways: in the arc of a game from the stands or a season from the box scores, in photos, or even in numbers. At Baseball Prospectus, we understand that statistics don't replace observation or any of baseball's stories, but complement everything else that makes the game so much fun.

What stats help us with is with patterns and precision, variance and value. This book can help you learn things you may not see from watching a game or hundred, whether it's the path of a career over time or the breadth of the entire MLB. We'd also never ask you to choose between our numbers and the experience of viewing a game from the cheap seats or the comfort of your home; our publication combines running the numbers with observations and wisdom from some of the brightest minds we can find. But if you *do* want to learn more about the numbers beyond what's on the backs of player jerseys, let us help explain.

Offense

At the end of this past year, we've revised our methodology for determining batting value. Long-time readers of Baseball Prospectus will notice that we've retired True Average in favor of a new metric: Deserved Runs Created Plus (DRC+). Developed by Jonathan Judge and our stats team, this statistic measures everything a player does at the plate–reaching base, hitting for power, making outs, and moving runners over–and puts it on a scale where 100 equals league-average performance. A DRC+ of 150 is terrific, a DRC+ of 100 is average, and a DRC+ of 75 means you better be an excellent defender.

DRC+ also does a better job than any of our previous metrics in taking contextual factors into account. The model adjusts for how the park affects performance, but also for things like the talent of the opposing pitcher, value of different types of batted-ball events, league, temperature, and other factors. It's able to describe a player's expected offensive contribution than any other statistic we've found over the years, and also does a better job of predicting future performance as well.

The other aspect of run-scoring is baserunning, which we quantify using Baserunning Runs. BRR not only records the value of stolen bases (or getting caught in the act), but also accounts for a runner's ability to go first to third on a single or advance on a fly ball.

Defense

Where offensive value is *relatively* easy to identify and understand, defensive value is ... not. Over the past dozen years, the sabermetric community has focused mostly on stats based on zone data: a real-live human person records the type of batted ball and estimated landing location, and models are created that give expected outs. From there, you can compare fielders' actual outs to those expected ones. Simple, right?

Unfortunately, zone data has two major issues. First, zone data is recorded by commercial data providers who keep the raw data private unless you pay for it. (All the statistics we build in this book and on our website use public data as inputs.) That hurts our ability to test assumptions or duplicate results. Second, over the years it has become apparent that there's quite a bit of "noise" in zone-based fielding analysis. Sometimes the conclusions drawn from zone data don't hold up to scrutiny, and sometimes the different data provided by different providers don't look anything alike, giving wildly different results. Sometimes the hard-working professional stringers or scorers might unknowingly inflict unconscious bias into the mix: for example good fielders will often be credited with more expected outs despite the data, and ballparks with high press boxes tend to score more line drives than ones with a lower press box.

Enter our Fielding Runs Above Average (FRAA). For most positions, FRAA is built from play-by-play data, which allows us to avoid the subjectivity found in many other fielding metrics. The idea is this: count how many fielding plays are made by a given player and compare that to expected plays for an average fielder at their position (based on pitcher ground-ball tendencies and batter handedness). Then we adjust for park and base-out situations.

When it comes to catchers, our methodology is a little different thanks to the laundry list of responsibilities they're tasked with beyond just, well, catching and throwing the ball. By now you've probably heard about "framing" or the art of making umpires more likely to call balls outside the strike zone for strikes. To put this into one tidy number, we incorporate pitch tracking data (for the years it exists) and adjust for important factors like pitcher, umpire, batter, and home-field advantage using a mixed-model approach. This grants us a number for how many strikes the catcher is personally adding to (or subtracting from) his pitchers' performance ... which we then convert to runs added or lost using linear weights.

Framing is one of the biggest parts of determining catcher value, but we also take into account blocking balls from going past, whether a scorer deems it a passed ball or a wild pitch. We use a similar approach–one that really benefits from the pitch tracking data that tells us what ends up in the dirt and what doesn't. We also include a catcher's ability to prevent stolen bases and how well they field balls in play, and *finally* we come up with our FRAA for catchers.

Pitching

Both pitching and fielding make up the half of baseball that isn't run scoring: run prevention. Separating pitching from fielding is a tough task, and most recent pitching analysis has branched off from Voros McCracken's famous (and controversial) statement, "There is little if any difference among major-league pitchers in their ability to prevent hits on balls hit in the field of play." The research of the analytic community has validated this to some extent, and there are a host of "defense-independent" pitching measures that have been developed to try and extricate the effect of the defense behind a hurler from the pitcher's work.

Our solution to this quandry is Deserved Run Average (DRA), our core pitching metric. DRA looks like earned run average (ERA), the tried-and-true pitching stat you've seen on every baseball broadcast or box score from the past century, but it's very different. To start, DRA takes an event-by-event look at what the pitchers does, and adjusts the value of that event based on different environmental factors like park, batter, catcher, umpire, base-out situation, run differential, inning, defense, home field advantage, pitcher role, and temperature. That mixed model gives us a pitcher's expected contribution, similar to what we do for our DRC+ model for hitters and FRAA model for catchers. (Oh, and we also consider the pitcher's effect on basestealing and on balls getting past the catcher.)

It's important to note that DRA is set to the scale of runs allowed per nine innings (RA9) instead of ERA, which makes DRA's scale slightly higher than ERA's. The reason for this is because ERA tends to overrate three types of pitchers:

1. Pitchers who play in parks where scorers hand out more errors. Official scorers differ significantly in the frequency at which they assign errors to fielders.
2. Ground-ball pitchers, because a substantial proportion of errors occur on grounders.
3. Pitchers who aren't very good. Better pitchers often allow fewer unearned runs than bad pitchers, because good pitchers tend to find ways to get out of jams.

Since the last time you picked up an edition of this book, we've also made a few minor changes to DRA to make it better. Recent research into "tunneling"–the act of throwing consecutive pitches that appear similar from a batter's point of view until after the swing decision point–data has given us a new contextual factor to account for in DRA: plate distance. This refers to the distance between successive pitches as they approach the plate, and while it has a smaller effect than factors like velocity or whiff rate, it still can help explain pitcher strikeout rate in our model.

New Pitching Metrics for 2019

We're including a few "new" pitching metrics for 2019's suite of Baseball Prospectus publications, but you may be familiar with them if you've spent time scouring the internet for stats.

Fastball Percentage

Our fastball percentage (FB%) statistic measures how frequently a pitcher throws a pitch classified as a "fastball," measured as a percentage of overall pitches thrown. We qualify three types of fastballs:

1. The traditional four-seam fastball;
2. The two-seam fastball or sinker;
3. "Hard cutters," which are pitches that have the movement profile of a cut fastball and are used as the pitcher's primary offering or in place of a more traditional fastball.

For example, a pitcher with a FB% of 67 throws any combination of these three pitches about two-thirds of the time.

Whiff Rate

Everybody loves a swing and a miss, and whiff rate (WHF) measures how frequently pitchers induce a swinging strike. To calculate WHF, we add up all the pitches thrown that ended with a swinging strike, then divide that number by a pitcher's total pitches thrown. Most often, high whiff rates correlate with high strikeout rates (and overall effective pitcher performance).

Called Strike Probability

Called Strike Probability (CSP) is a number that represents the likelihood that all of a pitcher's pitches will be called a strike while controlling for location, pitcher and batter handedness, umpire and count. Here's how it works: on each pitch, our model determines how many times (out of 100) that a similar pitch was called for a strike given those factors mentioned above, and when normalized

www.baseballprospectus.com

for each batter's strike zone. Then we average the CSP for all pitches thrown by a pitcher in a season, and that gives us the yearly CSP percentage you see in the stats boxes.

As you might imagine, pitchers with a higher CSP are more likely to work in the zone, where pitchers with a lower CSP are likely locating their pitches outside the normal strike zone, for better or for worse.

Projections

Many of you aren't turning to this book just for a look at what a player has done, but for a look at what a player is going to do: the PECOTA projections. PECOTA, initially developed by Nate Silver (who has moved on to greater fame as a political analyst), consists of three parts:

1. Major-league equivalencies, which use minor-league statistics to project how a player will perform in the major leagues;
2. Baseline forecasts, which use weighted averages and regression to the mean to estimate a player's current true talent level; and
3. Aging curves, which uses the career paths of comparable players to estimate how a player's statistics are likely to change over time.

With all those important things covered, let's take a look at what's in the book this year.

Team Prospectus

You bought this book to learn more about your favorite (or maybe least-favorite, who are we to judge?) team, so let's talk about them. After a thoughtful preview of the 2019 season, you'll be presented with our Team Prospectus. This outlines many of the key statistics for each team's 2018 season, as well as a very inviting stadium diagram.

First you'll find the Performance Graphs page. The first is the 2018 Hit List Ranking. This shows our Hit List Rank for the team on each day of the 2018 season and is intended to give you a picture of the ups and downs of the team's season, including their highest and lowest ranks of the year. Hit List Rank measures overall team performance and drives the Hit List Power Rankings at the baseballprospectus.com website.

The second graph is Committed Payroll and helps you see how the team's payroll has compared to the MLB and divisional average payrolls over time. Payroll figures are currents as of January 1, 2019; with so many free agents still unsigned as of this writing, the final 2018 figure will likely be significantly different for many teams. (In the meantime, you can always find the most current data at Baseball Prospectus' Cot's Baseball Contracts page.)

Statistical Introduction - xi

The third graph is Farm System Ranking and displays how the Baseball Prospectus prospect team has ranked the organization's farm system since 2007. It also indicates the highest and lowest ranks that the farm system achieved over that time.

We start the Team Performance page with the squad's unadjusted and third-order 2018 win-loss records, presented in divisional context. We then list the three highest performing hitters and pitchers by WARP for 2018. Beneath that are a host of other team statistics. **Pythag** presents an adjusted 2018 winning percentage, calculated by taking runs scored per game (**RS/G**) and runs allowed per game (**RA/G**) for the team, and running them through a version of Bill James' Pythagorean formula that was refined and improved by David Smyth and Brandon Heipp. (The formula is called "Pythagenpat," which is equally fun to type and to say.)

Next up is **DRC+**, described earlier, to indicate the overall hitting ability of the team either above or below league-average. Run prevention on the pitching side is covered by **DRA** (also mentioned earlier) and another metric: Fielding Independent Pitching (**FIP**), which calculates another ERA-like statistic based on strikeouts, walks, and home runs recorded. Defensive Efficiency Rating (**DER**) tells us the percentage of balls in play turned into outs for the team, and is a quick fielding shorthand that rounds out run prevention.

After that, we have several measures related to roster composition, as opposed to on-field performance. **B-Age** and **P-Age** tell us the average age of a team's batters and pitchers, respectively. **Salary** is the combined team payroll for all on-field players, and Doug Pappas' Marginal Dollars per Marginal Win (**M$/MW**) tells us how much money a team spent to earn production above replacement level.

Ending this batch of statistics is the number of disabled list days a team had over the season (**DL Days**) and the amount of salary paid to players on the disabled list (**$ on DL**); this final number is expressed as a percentage of total payroll.

Next to each of these stats, we've listed each team's MLB rank in that category from 1st to 30th. In this, 1st always indicates a positive outcome and 30th a negative outcome, except in the case of salary–1st is highest.

The Team Projections page is intended to convey the team's operational capacity entering the 2019 season. We start with the team's PECOTA projected record for 2019, again in divisional context. The +/- column indicates how many more or less wins the team is projected to get than they got in 2018. We then list the three highest projected hitters and pitchers by WARP for 2018. A brief farm system summary follows, with the team's top prospect and number of BP Top 101 Prospects. Finally, we list the key new players and departed players, along with their 2019 projected WARP.

Alex Bregman 3B

Born: 03/30/94 Age: 25 Bats: R Throws: R
Height: 6'0" Weight: 180 Origin: Round 1, 2015 Draft (#2 overall)

YEAR	TEAM	LVL	AGE	PA	R	2B	3B	HR	RBI	BB	K	SB	CS	AVG/OBP/SLG
2016	CCH	AA	22	285	54	16	2	14	46	42	26	5	3	.297/.415/.559
2016	FRE	AAA	22	83	17	6	0	6	15	5	12	2	1	.333/.373/.641
2016	HOU	MLB	22	217	31	13	3	8	34	15	52	2	0	.264/.313/.478
2017	HOU	MLB	23	626	88	39	5	19	71	55	97	17	5	.284/.352/.475
2018	HOU	MLB	24	705	105	51	1	31	103	96	85	10	4	.286/.394/.532
2019	HOU	MLB	25	675	96	38	3	23	78	73	107	12	4	.272/.359/.463

Breakout: 6% Improve: 52% Collapse: 5% Attrition: 2% MLB: 100%
Comparables: Anthony Rendon, David Wright, Pablo Sandoval

YEAR	TEAM	LVL	AGE	PA	DRC+	VORP	BABIP	BRR	FRAA	WARP
2016	CCH	AA	22	285	172	38.9	.286	1.6	SS(51): -3.4, 3B(11): 1.4	2.7
2016	FRE	AAA	22	83	161	10.0	.333	-1.2	SS(14): 2.1, LF(3): -0.1	0.8
2016	HOU	MLB	22	217	107	9.6	.317	0.5	3B(40): 0.9, SS(6): -0.1	1.1
2017	HOU	MLB	23	626	114	34.7	.311	-1.5	3B(132): 8.7, SS(30): -2.9	3.9
2018	HOU	MLB	24	705	150	72.6	.289	-1.6	3B(136): 5.4, SS(28): -0.4	7.4
2019	HOU	MLB	25	675	125	37.3	.295	0.0	3B 7, SS 0	4.6

After the projections page, we share a few items about the team's home ballpark. There's the aforementioned diagram of the park's dimensions (including distances to the outfield wall), a few important biographical facts about the stadium, a graphic showing the height of the wall from the left-field pole to the right-field pole, and a table showing three-year park factors for the stadium. The park factors are displayed as indexes where 100 is average, 110 means that the park inflates the statistic in question by 10 percent, and 90 means that the park deflates the statistic in question by 10 percent.

Following the ballpark page, we have a **Personnel** section that lists many of the important decision-makers and upper-level field and operations staff members for the franchise, as well as any former Baseball Prospectus staff members who are currently part of the organization.

Position Players

After all that information and a thoughtful bylined essay covering each team, we present our player comments. Each player is listed with the major-league team who employed him as of early January 2019. If a player changed teams after that point via free agency, trade, or any other method, you'll be able to find them in the book for their previous squad.

First, we cover biographical information (age is as of June 30, 2019) before moving onto the stats themselves. Our statistic columns include standard identifying information like **YEAR**, **TEAM**, **LVL** (level of affiliated play) and **AGE** before getting into the numbers. Next, we provide raw, unstranslated numbers like you might find on the back of your dad's baseball cards: **PA** (plate appearances), **R** (runs), **2B** (doubles), **3B** (triples), **HR** (home runs), **RBI** (runs batted in), **BB** (walks), **K** (strikeouts), **SB** (stolen bases) and **CS** (caught stealing). Then we have unadjusted "slash" statistics: **AVG** (batting average), **OBP** (on-base percentage) and **SLG** (slugging percentage).

Just below the stats box is **PECOTA** data, which is discussed further in a following section. After that, it's on to a pithy and always-informative comment written by a member of the Baseball Prospectus staff, before we cover more stats.

The second text box repeats YEAR, TEAM, LVL, AGE, and PA, then moves on to **DRC+** (Deserved Runs Created Plus), which we described earlier as total offensive expected contribution compared to the league average. Next, one of our oldest active metrics, **VORP** (Value Over Replacement Player), considers offensive production, position and plate appearances. In essence, it is the number of runs contributed beyond what a replacement-level player at the same position would contribute if given the same percentage of team plate appearances. VORP does not consider the quality of a player's defense.

BABIP (batting average on balls in play) tells us how often a ball in play fell for a hit, and can help us identify whether a batter may have been lucky or not ... but note that high BABIPs also tend to follow the great hitters of our time, as well as speedy singles hitters who put the ball on the ground.

The next item is **BRR** (Baserunning Runs), which covers all of a player's baserunning accomplishments which includes (but isn't limited to) swiped bags and failed attempts. Next is **FRAA** (Fielding Runs Above Average), which also includes the number of games previously played at each position noted in parentheses. Multi-position players have only their two most frequent positions listed here, but their total FRAA number reflects all positions played.

Our last column here is **WARP** (Wins Above Replacement Player). WARP estimates the total value of a player, which means for hitters it takes into account hitting runs above average (calculated using the DRC+ model), BRR and FRAA. Then, it makes an adjustment for positions played and gives the player a credit for plate appearances based upon the difference between "replacement level"¬–which is derived from the quality of players added to a team's roster after the start of the season¬–and the league average.

Catchers

Catchers are a special breed, and thus they have earned their own separate box which displays some of the defensive metrics that we've built just for them. As an example, let's check out J.T. Realmuto.

YEAR	TEAM	P. COUNT	FRM RUNS	BLK RUNS	THRW RUNS	TOT RUNS
2016	MIA	18935	-8.5	1.8	2.1	-5.6
2017	MIA	18959	5.3	1.7	1.0	9.1
2018	MIA	16399	-0.4	0.9	0.1	0.4
2019	PHI	18448	-1.4	1.5	0.7	0.8

The **YEAR** and **TEAM** columns match what you'd find in the other stat box. **P. COUNT** indicates the number of pitches thrown while the catcher was behind the plate, including swinging strikes, fouls, and balls in play. **FRM RUNS** is the total run value the catcher provided (or cost) his team by influencing the umpire to call strikes where other catchers did not. **BLK RUNS** expresses the total run value above or below average for the catcher's ability to prevent wild pitches and passed balls. **THRW RUNS** is calculated using a similar model as the previous two statistics, and it measures a catcher's ability to throw out basestealers but also to dissuade them from testing his arm in the first place. It takes into account factors like the pitcher (including his delivery and pickoff move) and baserunner (who could be as fast as Billy Hamilton or as slow as Yonder Alonso). **TOT RUNS** is the sum of all of the previous three statistics.

Pitchers

Let's give our pitchers a turn, using 2018 NL Cy Young winner Jacob deGrom as our example. Take a look at his first stat block: the first line and the **YEAR**, **TEAM**, **LVL** and **AGE** columns are the same as in the position player example earlier.

Here too, we have a series of columns that display raw, unadjusted statistics compiled by the pitcher over the course of a season: **W** (wins), **L** (losses), **SV** (saves), **G** (games pitched), **GS** (games started), **IP** (innings pitched), **H** (hits allowed) and **HR** (home runs allowed). Next we have two statistics that are rates: **BB/9** (walks per nine innings) and **K/9** (strikeouts per nine innings), before returning to the unadjusted **K** (strikeouts).

Next up is **GB%** (ground ball percentage), which is the percentage of all batted balls that were hit in the ground, including both outs and hits. Remember, this is based on observational data and subject to human error, so please approach this with a healthy dose of skepticism.

BABIP (batting average on balls in play) is calculated using the same methodology as it is for position players, but it often tells us more about a pitcher than it does a hitter. With pitchers, a high BABIP is often due to poor defense or bad luck, and can often be an indicator of potential rebound, and a low BABIP may be cause to expect performance regression. (A typical league-average BABIP is close to .290-.300.)

After a witty 150ish words on the player like only Baseball Prospectus's staff can provide, it's on to that second stat block, which repeats the YEAR, TEAM, LVL, and AGE columns. The metrics **WHIP** (walks plus hits per inning pitched) and **ERA**

San Diego Padres 2019

(earned run average) are old standbys: WHIP measures walks and hits allowed on a per-inning basis, while ERA measures earned runs on a nine-inning basis. Neither of these stats are translated or adjusted.

DRA (Deserved Run Average) was described at length earlier, and measures how many runs the pitcher "deserved" to allow per nine innings. Please note that since we lack all the data points that would make for a "real" DRA for minor-league events, the DRA displayed for minor league partial-seasons is based off of different data. (That data is a modified version of our cFIP metric, which you can find more information about on our website.)

Jacob deGrom   RHP
Born: 06/19/88   Age: 31   Bats: L   Throws: R
Height: 6'4"   Weight: 180   Origin: Round 9, 2010 Draft (#272 overall)

YEAR	TEAM	LVL	AGE	W	L	SV	G	GS	IP	H	HR	BB/9	K/9	K	GB%	BABIP
2016	NYN	MLB	28	7	8	0	24	24	148	142	15	2.2	8.7	143	47%	.312
2017	NYN	MLB	29	15	10	0	31	31	201[1]	180	28	2.6	10.7	239	48%	.305
2018	NYN	MLB	30	10	9	0	32	32	217	152	10	1.9	11.2	269	48%	.281
2019	NYN	MLB	31	13	9	0	31	31	186	145	18	2.3	10.7	221	46%	.286

Breakout: 8%   Improve: 29%   Collapse: 28%   Attrition: 6%   MLB: 85%
Comparables: Erik Bedard, A.J. Burnett, CC Sabathia

YEAR	TEAM	LVL	AGE	WHIP	ERA	DRA	WARP	MPH	FB%	WHF	CSP
2016	NYN	MLB	28	1.20	3.04	3.30	3.5	96.3	59.6	12.1	47.2
2017	NYN	MLB	29	1.19	3.53	3.02	5.7	97.2	55.5	14.5	49.5
2018	NYN	MLB	30	0.91	1.70	2.09	8.0	98.2	52.1	16.3	48.4
2019	NYN	MLB	31	1.02	2.91	3.23	3.9	96.6	54.5	14.8	48.2

Just like with hitters, **WARP** (Wins Above Replacement Player) is a total value metric that puts pitchers of all stripes on the same scale as position players. We use DRA as the primary input for our calculation of WARP. You might notice that relief pitchers (due to their limited innings) may have a lower WARP than you were expecting or than you might see in other WARP-like metrics. WARP does not take leverage into account, just the actions a pitcher performs and the expected value of those actions ... which ends up judging high-leverage relief pitchers differently than you might imagine given their prestige and market value.

MPH gives you the pitcher's 95th percentile velocity for the noted season, in order to give you an idea of what the *peak* fastball velocity a pitcher possesses. Since this comes from our pitch tracking data, it is not publicly available for minor-league pitchers.

Finally, we display the three new pitching metrics we described earlier. **FB%** (fastball percentage) gives you the percentage of fastballs thrown out of all pitches. **WhiffRt** (whiff rate) tells you the percentage of swinging strikes induced out of all pitches. **CS Prob** (called strike probability) expresses the likelihood of all pitches thrown to result in a called strike, after controlling for factors like handedness, umpire, pitch type, count, and location.

PECOTA

All players have PECOTA projections for 2019, as well as a set of other numbers that describe the performance of comparable players according to PECOTA. All projections for 2019 are for the player at the date we went to press in early January and are projected into the league and park context as indicated by the team abbreviation. All PECOTA projected statistics represent a player's projected major-league performance.

The numbers beneath the player's stats–Breakout, Improve, Collapse, Attrition–are part and parcel of the PECOTA projections. They estimate the likelihood of changes in performance relative to the player's previously-established level of production, based on the performance of comparable players:

Breakout Rate is the percent change that a player's production will improve by at least 20 percent relative to the weighted average of his performance over his most recent seasons.

Improve Rate is the percent chance that a player's production will improve at all relative to his baseline performance. A player who is expected to perform just the same as he has in the recent past will have an Improve Rate of 50 percent.

Collapse Rate is the percent chance that a position player's production will decline by at least 25 percent relative to his baseline performance.

Attrition Rate operates on playing time rather than performance. Specifically, it measures the likelihood that a player's playing time will decrease by at least 50 percent relative to his established level.

Breakout Rate and Collapse Rate can sometimes be counterintuitive for players who have already experienced a radical change in performance level. It's also worth noting that the projected decline in a player's rate performances might not be indicative of an expected decline in underlying ability or skill, but could just be an anticipated correction following a breakout season.

MLB% is the percentage of similar players who played in the major leagues in their relevant season.

The final pieces of information are the player's three highest-scoring comparable players as determined by PECOTA. All comparables represent a snapshot of how the listed player was performing at the same age as the current player, so if a 23-year-old pitcher is compared to Bartolo Colon, he's actually being compared to a 23-year-old Colon, not the version that pitched for the Rangers in 2018, nor to Colon's career as a whole.

A few points about pitcher projections. First, we aren't yet projecting peak velocity, so that column will be blank in the PECOTA lines. Second, projecting DRA is trickier than evaluating past performance, because it is unclear how deserving each pitcher will be of his anticipated outcomes. However, we know that another DRA-related statistic–contextual FIP or cFIP–estimates future run scoring very well. So for PECOTA, the projected DRA figures you see are based on the past cFIPs generated by the pitcher and comparable players over time, along with the other factors described above.

Lineouts

In each chapter's Lineouts section, you'll find abbreviated text comments, as well as most of same information you'd find in our full player comments. We limit the stats boxes in this section to only including the 2018 information for each player.

Exclusive Player Visualizations

In our constant battle to provide you with new and interesting baseball content you can't find anywhere else, we've added a trio of data visualizations to each hitter's entry in these books and a pair of visualizations for each pitcher.

For hitters, you'll find three new infographics. The first is each player's **Batted Ball Distribution**, which displays the five major sections of the field: LF (left), LCF (left center), CF (center), RCF (right center), and RF (right). The percentage indicated tells us what percentage of batted balls from that hitter fell within that part of the field during the 2018 season. We've also included the hitter's slugging percentage on balls in play (also called **SLGCON**) for that part of the field.

You'll also see two heatmaps: **Strike Zone vs LHP** and **Strike Zone vs RHP**. These heat maps represent a view of the strike zone from behind the catcher. Areas where there is a darker coloration represent the places where a higher percentage of pitches resulted in hits. In other words, the heatmap represents a hitter's "sweet spots" for getting hits against either left-handed or right-handed pitchers, depending on the image.

Pitchers get two images that help explain what their pitches look like from a hitter's perspective: **Pitch Shape vs LHH** and **Pitch Shape vs RHH**. These images show you the shape and the "tunneling" effect of each pitcher's offerings from the batter's perspective. For each type of pitch that a pitcher throws (represented by an indicator shape), there's a set of dots indicating the flight path, where each dot represents a 0.01-second interval. This maps the average trajectory and speed of an offering, ending where the ball crosses the plate. The solid black box represents the regular strike zone, while the gray contour lines indicate the range of locations that a pitcher typically works in.

Below the image, we provide a bit more detailed information about each pitcher's average offering in the **Pitch Types** box. Here, we also list each of the pitcher's major offerings under the **Type** column.

- **Fastballs** (which usually refers to the four-seam variation)
- **Sinkers** and/or two-seam fastballs
- **Cutters** (which could include "hard" cutters like cut fastballs and "soft" cutters that resemble hard sliders)
- **Changeups** (not including most splitters)
- **Splitters** (split-fingered pitches, forkballs, and some split-changes)
- **Sliders** and/or slurves
- **Curveballs** (including spike-curveballs and knuckle-curveballs, as well as some slurvy curves)
- **Slow curveballs** and/or eephus pitches
- **Knuckleballs**
- **Screwballs**

The **Freq** column indicates the percentage of overall pitches that fall into each of those type categories; if a pitcher has a 16.55% score for changeups, then that's the percent of all pitches that he throws as changeups. **Velo** is exactly what you think it is: the average miles per hour for each pitch type. **H Mov** is the number of inches of horizontal movement on the average pitch of that type, while **V Mov** is the number of inches of vertical movement on the average pitch of that type. (At Baseball Prospectus, we measure this over the long flight of the ball and include gravity into the V Mov number in order to give you the most realistic representation of what the pitch *actually* does.)

If you're wondering about the second number in brackets, that's the index for that velocity or movement compared to the league average. Like DRC+, a score of 100 means that the speed or movement is about the same as league average, while a higher score means that there's higher velocity or movement than the league average. Numbers below 100 indicate less velocity or movement than the league average.

Part 1: Team Analysis

Table for Two: Previewing the 2019 San Diego Padres

Sean Addis and Lance Brozdowski

LANCE BROZDOWSKI: Manny Machado signed with the San Diego Padres. My favorite part of that sentence is the evolution of "#PadresTwitter" since signing day. From shot-gunning beers to erecting monuments for Ron Fowler, the bar for celebration is sky high if this team wins a World Series in the next 10 seasons.

We at BP consider Machado a 3.5-WARP player for 2019 with a 122 DRC+. This puts him outside of the top 30 projected hitters, a threshold other some other industry leaders have Mr. San Diego north of. He jumps the Padres' projected win total from 76 to 79 wins, still three games back of the Diamondbacks, but not completely out of sight from the second National League wild card slot.

The Padres' average home attendance rose 12 percent between 2014 and 2015 when the team acquired Craig Kimbrel, Kemp and others for a scrambled push into contention. Now, some four years later, I ask you Sean: Will the Padres attendance jump more than 12 percent from last season with this deliberate push into contention and does Machado reconfigure the Padres window of contention?

SEAN ADDIS: I wouldn't be planning any immediate routes on Fifth Avenue anytime soon. But the euphoria of the Machado signing will send fans scrambling to the ticket office. It's an indication that this ownership and team wants to build a winner and is willing to continue to add the pieces necessary to give the beautiful city of San Diego, their first World Championship. Honestly, hats off to them for seeing an opportunity and playing the game the big bad New York Yankees have for years. Score one for the small markets!

Between the investment in Eric Hosmer (albeit too much), the extension of Will Myers, and now the addition of Machado, Padres management is effectively securing the talent to compliment a young core. Luis Urias, Francisco Mejia and eventually Fernando Tatis, Jr. will have this season to develop at the major league level and that'll be exciting to see, but how they quickly reach their potential will be the biggest question.

San Diego Padres 2019

The key to the Padres becoming serious contenders, besides maturation of the young position players, will be the development and future additions to the pitching staff. The addition of Garrett Richards was a shrewd move for 2020, but they'll need to add experienced starters to the rotation similar to the Hosmer/Machado additions. With improved infield defense and a cupboard full of prospects, maybe the Padres should return to their popular trade partner, the Toronto Blue Jays. They could swoop in and get the disgruntled, groundball machine (64% in 2018) and projected 2.3-WARP starter Marcus Stroman. Lance, how do you think they should improve the rotation and which young pitchers do you think will step up in 2019?

LANCE: I think the answer is hidden in the middle of the Padres PECOTA projections: Chris Paddack. He is projected to produce 0.5 WARP just like Robbie Erlin, Matt Strahm and Luis Perdomo, yet he's doing so with 60 to 80 less innings. His stats in the minor leagues are beyond dominant and the lack-of-a-third-pitch narrative will quickly fade if his curveball is merely average. I'd bet the shirt on my back he makes a hefty amount more than the five starts we have him projected for. Paddack is being thoroughly overlooked on nearly every outlet, and I expect his relevance to soar this spring.

The Padres also have Dinelson Lamet coming back from Tommy John surgery, Logan Allen, Cal Quantrill, Adrian Morejon, Michel Baez and the long-forgotten (and not yet 21-year-old) Anderson Espinoza waiting in the wings–all contenders to contribute this year or next. I'm still trying to convince myself going after starting pitching is a good move for them, and I understand I'm in the majority. If they're in it this year, it's for the second Wild Card. Next year the window should start to open and then catch some wind and fly wide open in 2021. Give me Stroman or Bauer in an arm-consolidation move, but otherwise let's see this well of young starting pitching flourish.

There's a chance that every time a pitcher looks to left field they're laying their eyes on a new player, right?

SEAN: Well, you'd have to believe that Wil Myers will see most of the time in left field, if healthy. After an injury-riddled season that limited him to 83 games and the signing of Hosmer last year, he played most of his games in left. However, the defensive metrics didn't like his performance with a -2.7 DRAA and -2.0 FRAA. The goal for Andy Green will be to get his bat in the lineup as frequent as possible, and hope he returns to his 2016-2017 glory.

The biggest challenge will be playing their abundance of outfielders consistently. Regulars Hunter Renfroe and Manuel Margot should be key pieces. Franmil Reyes also showcased a mixed bag of defense with +4.1 DRAA but -7.1 FRAA and great power (.218 ISO) in his limited debut last season. Margot is destined to play center field while Renfroe and Reyes will probably share playing time in right field and left field with Myers.

It could be quite possible Myers plays a small-scale "super utility" role this season. He could play both outfield corner positions and be moved from left to right based on level of difficulty of ballpark. He could even play some games at his best position first base and third base, where he saw some time late last season. This type of deployment could offset some of his inefficiencies out in the grass.

The outfield picture becomes even more crowded when you consider fourth outfielder Travis Jankowski and rookie Frenchy Cordero, who posted a slugging percentage of .603 in Triple-A as recently as 2017. I have to believe that unless there is an injury or trade, the Padres will want to get the young players full-time at-bats and therefore, some will start the season in the minors.

With a young team, it will be the veteran and character leadership the will be needed to help the young players adjust to he majors. Lance, who are your leadership guys in the Padres clubhouse?

LANCE: Is it weird to say a 26-year-old Machado can become a leader? I presume teams look to veteran leadership for roles of this nature, but with the youth emerging on the Padres, why not give the keys to a player who has grown substantially at the major league level? I think public perceptions of players often differ from their in-clubhouse demeanor. Maybe teammates love him? If they do and opposing team's fans don't, does it really matter to that clubhouse what other teams or fans think?

We need to give a little bit more attention to Cordero and Reyes as well. Cordero is only projected for 0.4 WARP, but that's over 231 plate appearances. He improved dramatically in a variety of areas last season compared to 2017. He started hitting the ball harder, with more line drives and improved his discipline at the plate with the ultimate benefit or more contact–good contact. All this and he's only 24 years old. If there is another swinging strike rate drop in 2019 and he maintains his exceptional bat speed, there's reason to think this tooled-up corner outfielder can barrel everything he sees.

Reyes enters Spring Training with no restrictions from a Winter League knee injury. He joins 33 other players as the only bats talented enough to hit a ball over 115 mph last season and has a power tool louder than Cordero's with a better ability to make contact. Sure, he's a liability in the outfield, but cheers to hiding poor defenders in left field if they continually wow at the plate.

Is there any improvement you really want to see a particular Padre make, Sean? Or a storyline that will make you turn off a Mike Trout at-bat to read about?

SEAN: I am excited to see what happens behind the plate. Austin Hedges was one of the best defensive catchers in all of baseball in 2018, and he had a down year compared to 2017. He ranked fourth in pitch framing (13.0), and fifth in FRAA (+11.8), after the 2017 out of this world FRAA of +34.1. Last season saw a major drop off in a couple of defensive metrics: throwing runs and blocking runs. But that could be attributed to the right elbow tendonitis he battled earlier in the season.

BP has him projected with a 2.5 BWARP and we know when he makes contact, he does so with power, as indicated by his .198 ISO in 2018. I think with the new revamped lineup, a year removed from his elbow injury and the opportunity to be rested with the emergence of Francisco Mejia, Hedges could be poised for a bigger season.

Speaking of Mejia, it will be great to see how he develops at the major league level under the tutelage of Hedges. As the BP team wrote, in the 2019 Prospect review of San Diego, he has a good arm, and his receiving has improved. The concern has been around his durability. But with Hedges doing the bulk of the catching I think the durability issue will be a non-factor. There has also been talk to play Mejia in the outfield, but that just could become a headache with all the bodies already trying to get at-bats.

Honestly, I am really intrigued what move Preller will make with all the excess talent he has at his disposal and the available salary dollars. If he channels his inner Boston President, Dave Dombrowski, it could get interesting and very busy. But we have been down that road before, I think this time he will take a more calculated approach.

Which acquisition, besides Machado, are you most intrigued to see perform this season? And which player are you looking to see improve?

LANCE: I'm going all the way back to July 2017 for my acquisition: Matt Strahm. He's 27 years old, with under 150 innings in his major league career, but he started relying on off-speed pitches more than his past indicated in 2018 and the results popped. I'm fascinated by pitchers right at their peak age per standard aging curves who develop a feel for a second breaking ball. Strahm had always been a curveball-dominant guy, but I think the lateral movement of his developing slider mixed in with his dominant changeup will allow him to neutralize right-handed hitters and even out his natural splits. If he's the team's most productive starting pitcher by the end of the season, I would not be surprised. I think that's my hottest take so far and one I'll stand by.

I might be low on Mejia compared to others. I think they made the right move by flipping saves for a prospect of this caliber, but even with his improving skills behind the plate, I don't see a universe where he's even splitting time with another catcher. He's a fill-in at best for me. With the Machado move, the left side will be clogged by Tatis Jr. and the multi-million-dollar man, leaving Mejia with little room to showcase his arm from the infield. So does he move to the outfield to mix himself in with the plethora of power-hitting assets? Where the Padres fit him in is almost as important as his production.

Do you have any final thoughts, Sean? How about a few predictions to close this out? Give me the Padres 2019 record, breakout talent and underperformer.

I'll predict 81-81, with Chris Paddack as the team's breakout talent and Mejia as the team's underperformer.

SEAN: Preller has the opportunity to go in many directions and it will be interesting how he uses the available salary and prospect capital to turn this team into a perennial contender. Transactions are exciting, but I think he should take a cautious approach. Spend this season determining the pieces he wants to build around and those he can use to acquire the other necessary pieces.

I will be more conservative with my prediction 78-84, with Hunter Renfroe having a breakout season while Manuel Margot being the biggest underperformer.

Performance Graphs

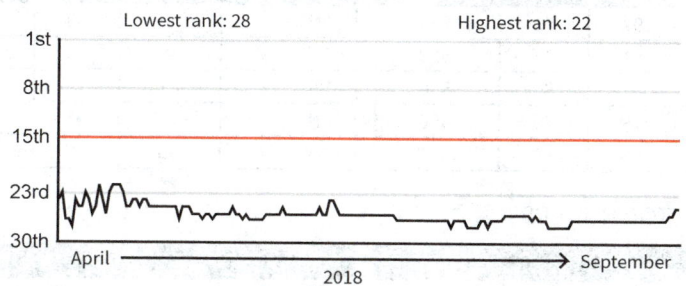

2018 Hit List Ranking

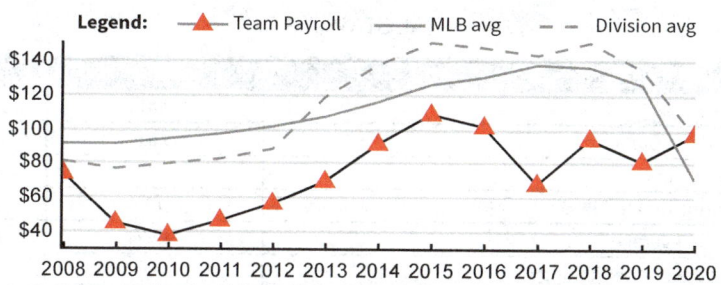

Committed Payroll (in millions)

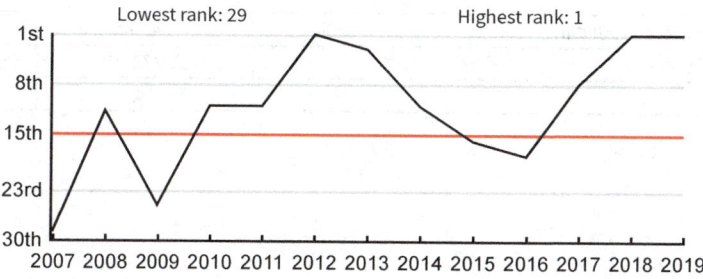

Farm System Ranking

2018 Team Performance

ACTUAL STANDINGS

Team	W	L	Pct
LAN	92	71	.564
COL	91	72	.558
ARI	82	80	.506
SFN	73	89	.450
SDN	**66**	**96**	**.407**

THIRD-ORDER STANDINGS

Team	W	L	Pct
LAN	105	58	.644
COL	88	75	.539
ARI	87	75	.537
SFN	71	91	.438
SDN	**66**	**96**	**.407**

TOP HITTERS

Player	WARP
Austin Hedges	2.1
Hunter Renfroe	2
Wil Myers	0.6

TOP PITCHERS

Player	WARP
Robbie Erlin	2.6
Joey Lucchesi	2.3
Kirby Yates	2.2

VITAL STATISTICS

Statistic Name	Value	Rank
Pythagenpat	.401	25th
Runs Scored per Game	3.81	28th
Runs Allowed per Game	4.73	21st
Deserved Runs Created Plus	79	30th
Deserved Run Average	4.52	19th
Fielding Independent Pitching	4.06	16th
Defensive Efficiency Rating	.695	27th
Batter Age	26.8	3rd
Pitcher Age	27.7	13th
Salary	$94.0M	25th
Marginal $ per Marginal Win	$4.6M	12th
Disabled List Days	$1,272.0M	19th
$ on DL	7%	1st

2019 Team Projections

PROJECTED STANDINGS

Team	W	L	Pct	+/-
LAN	93	69	.574	+1
COL	84	78	.518	-7
ARI	81	81	.500	-1
SDN	**79**	**83**	**.487**	**+13**
SFN	73	89	.450	0

TOP PROJECTED HITTERS

Player	WARP
Manny Machado	3.6
Austin Hedges	2.5
Wil Myers	2.4

TOP PROJECTED PITCHERS

Player	WARP
Joey Lucchesi	1.8
Garrett Richards	1.1
Matt Strahm	1.0

FARM SYSTEM REPORT

Top Prospect	Number of Top 101 Prospects
Fernando Tatis Jr., #3	9

KEY DEDUCTIONS

Player	WARP
Clayton Richard	0.8
Freddy Galvis	0.5

KEY ADDITIONS

Player	WARP
Manny Machado	3.6
Garrett Richards	1.1
Ian Kinsler	0.9

Team Personnel

EVP, General Manager
A.J. Preller

VP, Assistant General Manager
Fred Uhlman Jr.

Assistant General Manager
Josh Stein

Director, Baseball Operations
Nick Ennis

Manager
Andy Green

BP Alumni
David Cameron

Petco Park Stats

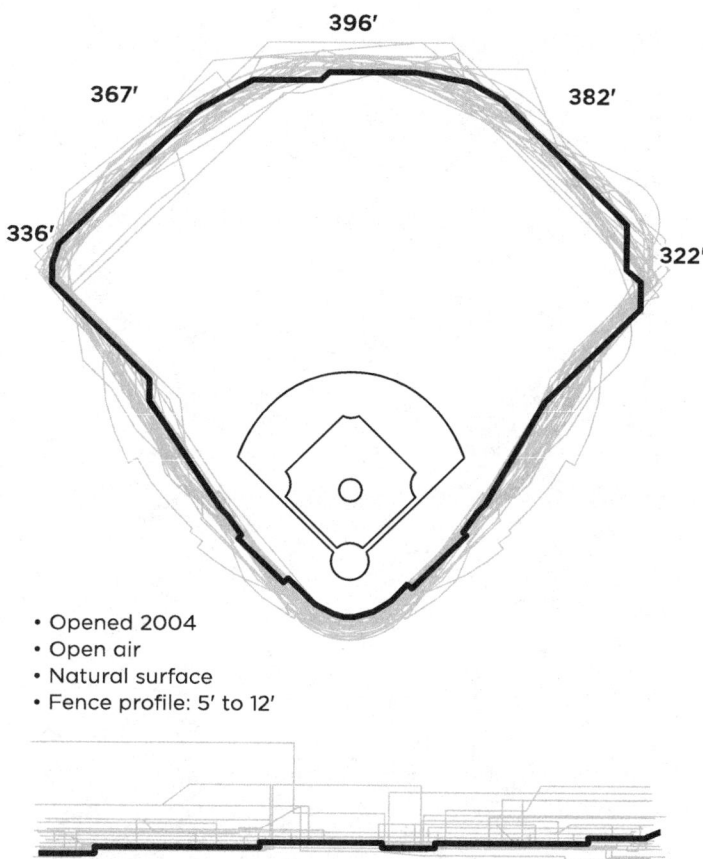

- Opened 2004
- Open air
- Natural surface
- Fence profile: 5' to 12'

Three-Year Park Factors

Runs	Runs/RH	Runs/LH	HR/RH	HR/LH
98	99	96	97	91

Padres Team Analysis

The 2019 season will mark fifty years of National League baseball in San Diego. Five decades from Nate Colbert to Tony Gwynn to Chase Headley to, well, Chase Headley again. Hard to believe right? They grow up so fast. It feels like just yesterday that Dick Selma was walking out to the mound to throw the first pitch in Padres franchise history glaring out from under the brim of his brown and yellow cap at a half-full San Diego Stadium. Looking on from the home dugout as Selma tossed a complete game victory was Preston Gomez, the first full-time Latino manager in MLB history. Baseball in San Diego. The future held endless possibility.

No man could have felt that possibility more tangibly than the Padres' owner, C. Arnholt Smith. The tall self-made millionaire from Walla Walla, Washington had risen from bank teller to bank owner. They called him Mr. San Diego. It feels like just yesterday that Smith, deep into all sorts of legal trouble after just a few years as a baseball owner, was enlisting the help of his friend, the recently impeached President Richard M. Nixon, in a desperate attempt to sell the Padres to prospective buyers in Washington D.C.

It almost ended right there. In 1974, Topps printed a set of cards that said, instead of San Diego Padres: Washington (NL). The new team was going to be called the Washington Stars. They even made up uniforms. That could have been it. But, as we know, it wasn't. So let's take a moment to appreciate the Padres at 50. The mere existence of this franchise—the last remaining major sports team in San Diego!—is something of a miracle. And it's even more impressive when you consider how terrible they have been.

In fifty years, the Padres have put up:

- 14 winning seasons
- 2 .500 seasons
- 34 losing seasons.

They have made the playoffs just five times, including in 2005 when they won the NL West despite going 82-80. They have made the World Series twice: in 1984 and 1998. Both times they lost convincingly despite the best efforts of Tony Gwynn who hit a combined .371 over nine games.

San Diego Padres 2019

Two of the Padres' fellow 1969 expansion clubs, the Montreal Expos and Seattle Pilots no longer exist. The Pilots only lasted a season before heading to Milwaukee. So all things considered, fifty years of mostly uneventful baseball really is an achievement. The on-field product might have been largely mediocre, but simply existing through all that mediocrity—well, that is a triumph.

Back in 1974, the Padres were rescued by a court injunction, and then by a fast food millionaire. C. Arnholt Smith was forced to sell the team, and the man who stepped in to buy it was McDonald's founder Ray Kroc, who made an immediate impression. During the eighth inning of his very first home game as owner, Kroc commandeered the public address system and declared, "I have never seen such stupid ballplaying in my life."

This scene, which did not make the Michael Keaton biopic, basically sums up the philosophical quandary that is the Padres. On one hand, it's great that there is a baseball team in San Diego. On the other, isn't it fair for Padres fans to ask for something better than stupid ballplaying? Doesn't the city of San Diego deserve something more than fourth place in the NL West, and the specter of a good team somewhere on the horizon?

If Ray Kroc was the first savior of the Padres, Tony Gwynn was the second. No team's legacy is as singularly defined by one player, locally or nationally. All due respect to Trevor Hoffman, Dave Winfield, Adrian Gonzalez, Randy Jones, Fred McGriff, Roberto Alomar, Ken Caminiti et. al but San Diego baseball is, and always has been Tony Gwynn. He has more than twice as many plate appearances in the uniform as the next closest Padre (that would be Randy Templeton).

But the thing about Tony Gwynn is that for as wonderful as he was—as a ballplayer and a person—he was one man. As Mike Trout can tell you, one man does not a baseball franchise make. The two times the Padres made the World Series, it was because they surrounded Gwynn with good players. In 1984 it was a dominant bullpen led by Goose Gossage, Dave Dravecky, and Craig Lefferts; in 1998 it was a balanced lineup (as Sosa and McGwire mashed their way into the record books, Greg Vaughn hit the quietest 50 homers in baseball history), an out-of-his-mind Kevin Brown, and an unstoppable Trevor Hoffman.

The Padres of today don't have a Tony Gwynn or a Trevor Hoffman or even a Greg Vaughn to buoy the franchise with star power and staying power. Although, if you are inclined, you can squint at Eric Hosmer and see the vague outline of Wally Joyner. Ever since general manager AJ Preller U-turned after his initial let's-go-crazy stab at contention in 2015, his teams have been Spangenberg-and-Jankowski-ing their way to 90-loss seasons. Last year, they lost 96.

"From a lineup standpoint," said Preller in a radio interview shortly after the conclusion of 2018 World Series, "it wasn't the '27 Yankees we ran out." But what the Padres have, in addition to a lovely, understated downtown ballpark, is potential. Not the squishy, ultimately meaningless notion of potential that C.

Arnholt Smith sold his investors on before going to jail for tax fraud—but the real thing. They have a bunch of really good, and really fun young ballplayers with the capacity to become a really good, and really fun young team.

Yeah, it's easy to say that. It's easy to read all the professional prospect watchers and draw the line between a "loaded system" that is "stocked with talent" and a successful major league team. Obviously it doesn't work that way. Obviously not all the players fans are dreaming about now will become part of the next winning Padres team, or hell, the first World Series winning Padres team. After all, they have a billion corner outfielders. Manuel Margot, their leadoff man of the future, struggled mightily in 2018. Hosmer's contract is massive. They have about twenty starting pitching prospects and two actual starting pitchers.

But the signs are there. After years of plodding along, Hunter Renfroe and Austin Hedges took meaningful steps in the direction of repeatable MLB success last year. It's a *good* thing that Renfroe will have to battle for continued playing time with Myers and with rookie outfielders Franmil Reyes and Franchy Cordero, who both look like players too. It's a *good* thing that Hedges will have to compete with Francisco Mejia, the prospect acquired from Cleveland in last season's Brad Hand trade. All of a sudden the Padres' depth chart problem is that they actually have depth. Plus, despite trading Hand, they bring back one of the best bullpens in the majors. Kirby Yates and Craig Stammen were dominant last season. If the Padres are good, Yates and Stammen will anchor a bullpen that will be crucial to their success. If the Padres are bad again, they will probably be flipped for more prospects.

More prospects—which at this point might be redundant. It's too early to credit Preller for a successful rebuild, but there's something beautiful and balanced about how the Padres' farm system, baseball's deepest, has come together. There have been the usual high draft picks that follow repeated losing, like the touted lefty Mackenzie Gore. There have been big international signings like Cuban pitching prospects Michel Baez and Adrian Morejon, and second baseman Luis Urias out of Mexico. (Signings that vindicate the Padres' efforts to claim an identity as a scouting savvy, internationally-minded franchise.) And most importantly, there have been trades.

Preller, who caught flack for his seemingly reckless dealing when he first came on board, has turned in some masterworks in the intervening years. The crown jewel of the Padres system is shortstop Fernando Tatis Jr—the kind of player who you only need to look at once to understand is special. He's still a teenager. The Padres got him for James Shields. Chris Paddack, a rising star who has never pitched above Double-A, but whom projection systems see as their best starting pitcher right now, came over from the Marlins in exchange for a 39-year-old Fernando Rodney. Mejia came in the Hand trade. The list goes on and on: Logan Allen, Anderson Espinoza, Josh Naylor.

San Diego Padres 2019

The Padres have managed to build their farm system without totally sacrificing culture at the major league level. Yes, the teams have been lousy, and yes the last five decades have resulted in very low institutional expectations, but San Diego has not tanked like Houston or Chicago. They went from being a bad team, to a bad team with a purpose, tending carefully, patiently to its soil, waiting for a garden to grow. (Perhaps this speaks to how little pressure the organization actually faces). Manager Andy Green is by all accounts forward-thinking and liked by all. If you watch the Padres, you get the sense that he is teasing out new strategies, working to develop his young players. What you don't get, is the sense that the Padres will go the way of the Cubs, Astros, and Braves, and fire their manager when it's time to compete. Rather, it appears they are building something with Green, sort of like (horrible cross-sport metaphor alert) the NBA's Philadelphia 76ers did with Brett Brown.

Which brings us to 2019. This is the year, Preller has said, that the Padres expect to take a step forward. Perhaps it will be led by Tatis, who is the only player in the system who makes you think, hmm, okay, maybe somebody *can* inherit Gwynn's mantle. Or perhaps this is simply the year that the explosive talent of Tatis and Urias and Paddack, and the still simmering potential of Margot, Reyes, Cordero, and Joey Lucchesi begins to coalesce. The Padres may not be a contender right now—but they can and should begin to resemble one.

Is it likely that now, fifty years into their existence, the core of the first Padres World Series winner is finally taking shape? If we've learned anything from Dick Selma and C. Arnholt Smith, it should be that the answer to this question is a resounding no. But it is possible: more possible than it has been since Gwynn was spraying line drives around Jack Murphy Stadium. The time is always right for appreciating the triumph of the Padres existence. But now the time is also right for fans to finally expect something more than stupid ballplaying, and more than optimism about the farm system.

And hell, they have Eric Hosmer. These Padres may not be the '27 Yankees. But maybe they can look to the only other surviving franchise from the expansion class of 1969. Maybe the '15 Kansas City Royals are within dreaming distance.

—Eric Nusbaum is a freelance writer and former editor at VICE Sports.

Part 2: Player Analysis

Franchy Cordero LF

Born: 09/02/94 Age: 24 Bats: L Throws: R
Height: 6'3" Weight: 175 Origin: International Free Agent, 2011

YEAR	TEAM	LVL	AGE	PA	R	2B	3B	HR	RBI	BB	K	SB	CS	AVG/OBP/SLG
2016	LEL	A+	21	322	47	16	8	5	35	19	83	11	8	.286/.339/.444
2016	SAN	AA	21	264	31	8	8	6	19	17	67	12	6	.306/.356/.478
2017	SDN	MLB	22	99	15	3	3	3	9	6	44	1	1	.228/.276/.424
2017	ELP	AAA	22	419	68	21	18	17	64	23	118	15	4	.326/.369/.603
2018	SDN	MLB	23	154	19	5	1	7	19	14	55	5	2	.237/.307/.439
2019	SDN	MLB	24	231	28	10	3	8	28	16	75	6	2	.242/.300/.431

Breakout: 14% Improve: 47% Collapse: 12% Attrition: 28% MLB: 70%
Comparables: David Dahl, Randal Grichuk, Trayvon Robinson

To call Cordero a shaky defender is to say Ignatius Reilly was a lousy frankfurter salesman; it's true, but also blandly understated. Last year, Cordero slipped and fell on his butt trying to field a single, clanged a flyball off his knee and somehow parlayed 70 speed into a 40 glove. As has long been the case, there's a canyon between his raw abilities and how they translate in games. Cordero can hit a ball 500 feet and run faster than just about anyone in the organization but he hasn't figured out how to productively apply those tools with any consistency. Instead, he'll follow up a four-hit weekend with a four-strikeout game, a nifty sliding catch with a slide that distinctly *prevents* a catch. Cordero isn't too old for a breakthrough, though he's more likely to become the league's toolsiest extra outfielder than a future regular.

YEAR	TEAM	LVL	AGE	PA	DRC+	VORP	BABIP	BRR	FRAA	WARP
2016	LEL	A+	21	322	98	21.4	.381	3.1	CF(68): -3.9, RF(2): 0.5	0.1
2016	SAN	AA	21	264	131	20.8	.401	-0.7	CF(59): 3.1	1.4
2017	SDN	MLB	22	99	54	3.8	.400	1.2	CF(25): 0.8, LF(1): -0.1	0.0
2017	ELP	AAA	22	419	116	37.2	.431	1.7	CF(61): -2.5, LF(22): 1.5	1.7
2018	SDN	MLB	23	154	72	4.6	.338	0.6	LF(22): 0.4, CF(11): -1.3	-0.2
2019	SDN	MLB	24	231	87	5.3	.325	0.7	CF -2, RF 0	0.3

Franchy Cordero, continued

Batted Ball Distribution

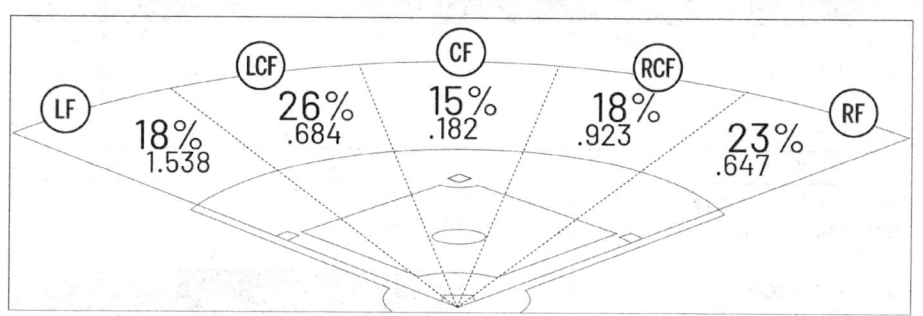

Strike Zone vs LHP **Strike Zone vs RHP**

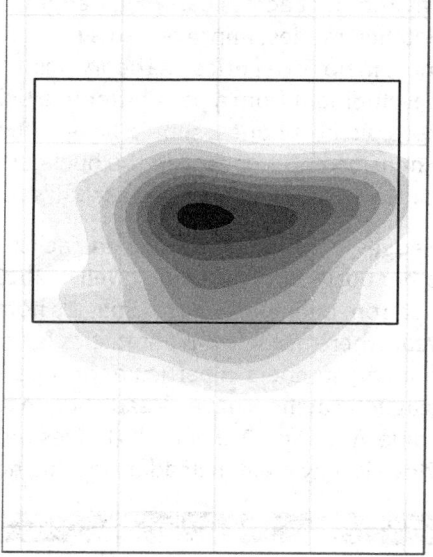

Austin Hedges C

Born: 08/18/92 Age: 26 Bats: R Throws: R
Height: 6'1" Weight: 206 Origin: Round 2, 2011 Draft (#82 overall)

YEAR	TEAM	LVL	AGE	PA	R	2B	3B	HR	RBI	BB	K	SB	CS	AVG/OBP/SLG
2016	ELP	AAA	23	334	55	20	1	21	82	13	51	1	1	.326/.353/.597
2016	SDN	MLB	23	26	2	1	0	0	1	0	7	0	1	.125/.154/.167
2017	SDN	MLB	24	417	36	17	0	18	55	23	122	4	1	.214/.262/.398
2018	SDN	MLB	25	326	29	14	2	14	37	21	90	3	0	.231/.282/.429
2019	SDN	MLB	26	347	40	16	1	13	42	22	85	3	1	.239/.292/.418

Breakout: 14% Improve: 60% Collapse: 9% Attrition: 8% MLB: 95%
Comparables: Jarrod Saltalamacchia, Wilin Rosario, Mike Zunino

For years, scouts gushed about Hedges's defense, wistfully saying he could be a franchise catcher, "if only he could hit..." In 2018, he finally hit. Amidst a slightly lower run scoring environment across baseball, Hedges notched modest improvements in most major categories. In theory, his

YEAR	TEAM	P. COUNT	FRM RUNS	BLK RUNS	THRW RUNS	TOT RUNS
2016	SDN	901	-0.3	0.2	0.0	2.1
2017	SDN	15353	28.0	1.3	2.2	30.3
2018	ELP	784	0.4	0.0	0.0	0.4
2018	SDN	11915	13.0	0.1	-0.4	12.6
2019	SDN	13091	15.2	0.7	0.3	16.2

development from a poor hitter to a below-average one with enough pop to keep pitchers honest should have sufficiently cleared the path to a contract extension and a decade in the bucket for San Diego. Instead, the Padres traded for Francisco Mejia, one of baseball's top catching prospects.

Hedges is the more established backstop and Mejia has already seen time at other positions; if both play well in 2019, it's the import who will have to move out from behind the plate. Still, it's notable that San Diego made this trade in a year where his defensive statistics fell from stratospheric to merely excellent. His framing numbers in particular dropped, and there's evidence that the rest of the league's catchers have already begun to narrow the gap, sapping some of his value. As far as 2019 goes, if Hedges returns to form, the job is his. But if the glove is only great instead of special, he may well lose out to Mejia.

YEAR	TEAM	LVL	AGE	PA	DRC+	VORP	BABIP	BRR	FRAA	WARP
2016	ELP	AAA	23	334	140	28.3	.329	-0.4	C(73): 5.2	2.9
2016	SDN	MLB	23	26	66	-2.7	.167	-0.1	C(7): 0.0	0.0
2017	SDN	MLB	24	417	75	8.3	.260	0.6	C(115): 34.1	4.2
2018	SDN	MLB	25	326	88	7.9	.280	-2.1	C(83): 11.8	2.1
2019	SDN	MLB	26	347	89	11.4	.283	-0.2	C 15	2.5

Austin Hedges, continued

Batted Ball Distribution

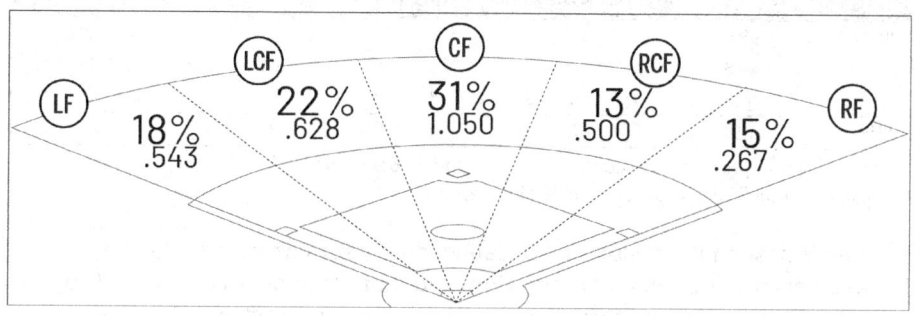

Strike Zone vs LHP   **Strike Zone vs RHP**

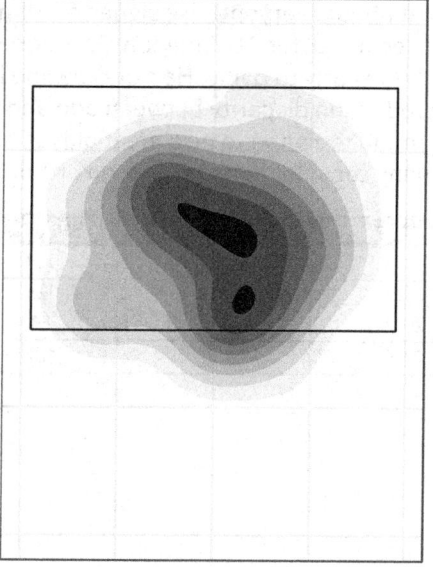

Eric Hosmer 1B

Born: 10/24/89 Age: 29 Bats: L Throws: L
Height: 6'4" Weight: 225 Origin: Round 1, 2008 Draft (#3 overall)

YEAR	TEAM	LVL	AGE	PA	R	2B	3B	HR	RBI	BB	K	SB	CS	AVG/OBP/SLG
2016	KCA	MLB	26	667	80	24	1	25	104	57	132	5	3	.266/.328/.433
2017	KCA	MLB	27	671	98	31	1	25	94	66	104	6	1	.318/.385/.498
2018	SDN	MLB	28	677	72	31	2	18	69	62	142	7	4	.253/.322/.398
2019	SDN	MLB	29	639	85	27	3	20	70	62	121	6	3	.271/.344/.434

Breakout: 7% Improve: 55% Collapse: 13% Attrition: 8% MLB: 97%
Comparables: Don Baylor, Cesar Cedeno, Ted Kluszewski

Hosmer is baseball's version of J.D. Salinger, in that there's a sizable gap between his production and reputation, and that it's uncouth to say so. The disconnect lurks at every turn. Despite shaky defensive metrics, he's always been considered a premier first baseman, and has won four Gold Gloves. He made the All-Star team and took home a trophy for the game's MVP award in a season where he wasn't much better than a replacement level player. And when just about everyone else signed for dimes on the dollar last winter, Hosmer inked a deal for $144 million. For Padres fans worried that Hosmer is a lemon, it's too early to panic. He's only 29 and has always had a weirdly large production disparity between odd and even years. While he hits the ball on the ground too often to be a great player, he's a decent bet to remind us why so many consider him a very good one in 2019.

YEAR	TEAM	LVL	AGE	PA	DRC+	VORP	BABIP	BRR	FRAA	WARP
2016	KCA	MLB	26	667	109	7.6	.301	0.1	1B(154): -2.2	1.4
2017	KCA	MLB	27	671	126	35.1	.351	-1.3	1B(157): 0.6	3.0
2018	SDN	MLB	28	677	84	-1.8	.302	-2.6	1B(157): 7.8	0.1
2019	SDN	MLB	29	639	107	17.5	.312	-0.6	1B -2	1.7

Eric Hosmer, continued

Batted Ball Distribution

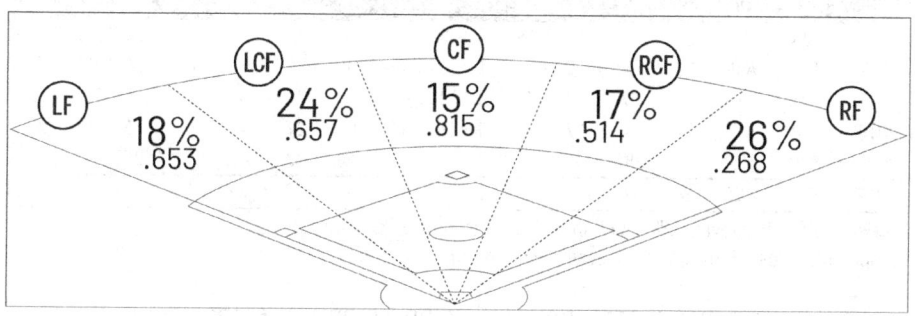

Strike Zone vs LHP   Strike Zone vs RHP

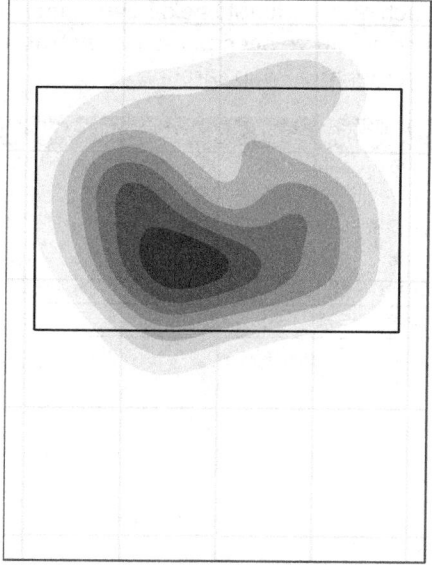

Travis Jankowski RF

Born: 06/15/91   Age: 28   Bats: L   Throws: R
Height: 6'2"   Weight: 185   Origin: Round 1, 2012 Draft (#44 overall)

YEAR	TEAM	LVL	AGE	PA	R	2B	3B	HR	RBI	BB	K	SB	CS	AVG/OBP/SLG
2016	SDN	MLB	25	383	53	13	2	2	12	42	100	30	12	.245/.332/.313
2017	ELP	AAA	26	157	20	5	1	0	11	18	28	8	1	.266/.350/.317
2017	SDN	MLB	26	87	10	2	0	0	1	9	28	4	0	.187/.282/.213
2018	ELP	AAA	27	94	17	4	0	1	11	11	21	4	3	.363/.452/.450
2018	SDN	MLB	27	387	45	12	3	4	17	37	73	24	7	.259/.332/.346
2019	SDN	MLB	28	98	11	3	1	2	9	9	22	5	2	.241/.320/.368

Breakout: 3%   Improve: 45%   Collapse: 5%   Attrition: 20%   MLB: 87%
Comparables: Joey Gathright, Tony Gwynn, Eric Young

Jankowski is a man out of his time. Called up a month after the unofficial start of the Juiced Ball Era, he's been among baseball's feeblest hitters ever since: Just one regular in that span has a lower slugging percentage and only a handful of guys have fewer home runs. Jankowski still has his uses, but you wonder how much more valuable he'd have been a few decades ago, when his slash-n-dash style would've been perfect on Astroturf. Perhaps he and Jerry Turner can get together and swap careers.

YEAR	TEAM	LVL	AGE	PA	DRC+	VORP	BABIP	BRR	FRAA	WARP
2016	SDN	MLB	25	383	71	10.0	.343	7.1	CF(87): -2.2, RF(22): -0.5	0.3
2017	ELP	AAA	26	157	73	1.2	.333	0.1	CF(22): -1.7, LF(7): -0.3	-0.4
2017	SDN	MLB	26	87	53	-3.1	.298	0.9	LF(19): -0.4, CF(4): 0.3	-0.2
2018	ELP	AAA	27	94	113	8.8	.483	1.5	CF(20): 2.5	0.7
2018	SDN	MLB	27	387	79	8.3	.319	4.5	RF(58): 3.3, CF(34): -1.7	0.4
2019	SDN	MLB	28	98	75	1.6	.299	0.5	CF 0, RF 1	0.2

Travis Jankowski, continued

Batted Ball Distribution

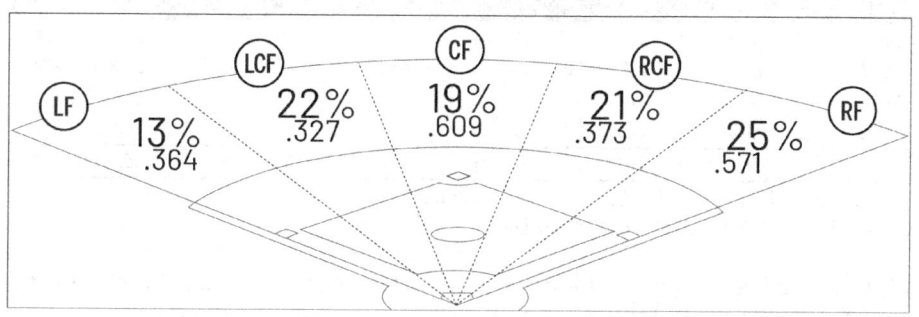

Strike Zone vs LHP   Strike Zone vs RHP

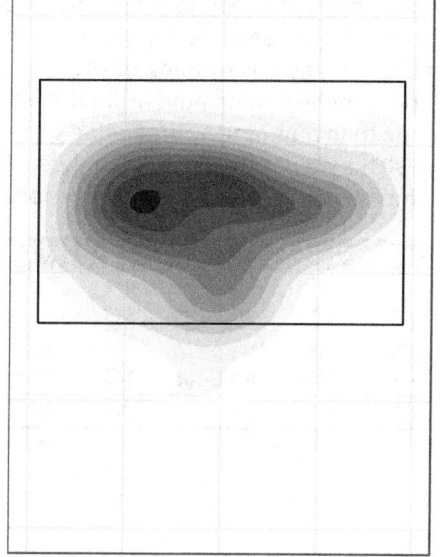

San Diego Padres 2019

Ian Kinsler 2B
Born: 06/22/82   Age: 37   Bats: R   Throws: R
Height: 6'0"   Weight: 200   Origin: Round 17, 2003 Draft (#496 overall)

YEAR	TEAM	LVL	AGE	PA	R	2B	3B	HR	RBI	BB	K	SB	CS	AVG/OBP/SLG
2016	DET	MLB	34	679	117	29	4	28	83	45	115	14	6	.288/.348/.484
2017	DET	MLB	35	613	90	25	3	22	52	55	86	14	5	.236/.313/.412
2018	ANA	MLB	36	391	49	20	0	13	32	30	40	9	4	.239/.304/.406
2018	BOS	MLB	36	143	17	6	0	1	16	10	24	7	3	.242/.294/.311
2019	SDN	MLB	37	218	30	11	1	6	23	18	35	5	2	.262/.332/.421

Breakout: 0%   Improve: 14%   Collapse: 21%   Attrition: 19%   MLB: 64%
Comparables: Del Pratt, Jerry Hairston, Mark Ellis

We should all feel happy that Kinsler, a Damn Fine Baseballer, was finally able to grab a ring with Boston last season after close calls with Texas and Detroit earlier in his career. It likely came at the perfect time, as it's tough to see a contender trusting him again. The once-dynamic talent is down to one remaining skill: defense. Our metrics may not love him, but that didn't stop him from winning his second Gold Glove. About that bat, though. Kinsler posted a lower ISO than Sean Rodriguez and a lower OBP than the ambulatory remains of Chase Utley. His running days are also behind him, as evidenced by his World Series pinch-running adventure that more closely resembled a Billy Joel drive home than anything approaching good base running. Could the 36-year-old sneak his way onto a roster as a defensive-minded bench piece? Sure. But at this point he'd be miscast as anything more.

YEAR	TEAM	LVL	AGE	PA	DRC+	VORP	BABIP	BRR	FRAA	WARP
2016	DET	MLB	34	679	123	40.2	.314	4.7	2B(151): 3.0	4.8
2017	DET	MLB	35	613	102	9.0	.244	4.7	2B(135): 1.0	2.6
2018	ANA	MLB	36	391	97	8.1	.237	-0.9	2B(91): 4.0	1.4
2018	BOS	MLB	36	143	97	-3.1	.287	0.6	2B(37): -1.3	0.3
2019	SDN	MLB	37	218	104	9.9	.287	0.1	2B 0	0.9

Ian Kinsler, continued

Batted Ball Distribution

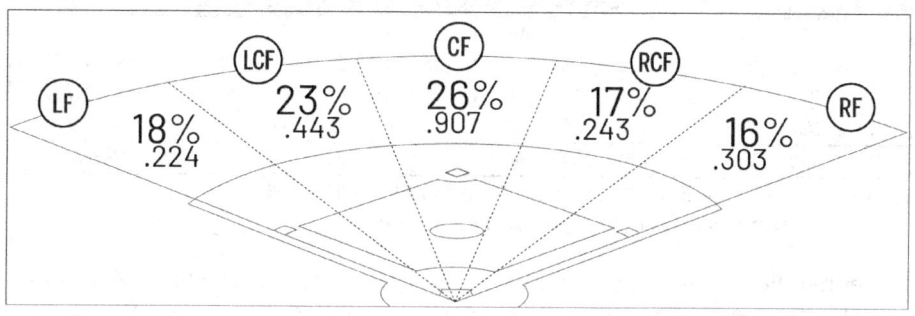

Strike Zone vs LHP **Strike Zone vs RHP**

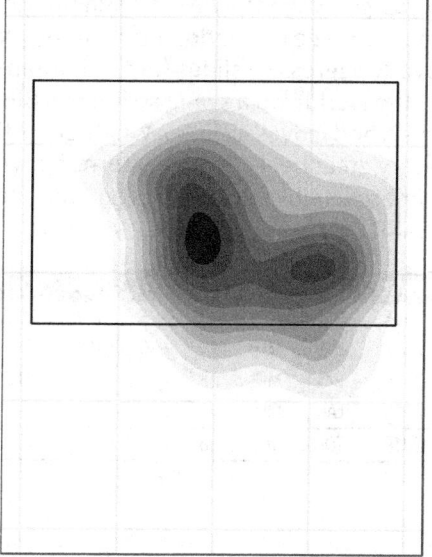

San Diego Padres 2019

Manny Machado 3B

Born: 07/06/92 Age: 26 Bats: R Throws: R
Height: 6'3" Weight: 185 Origin: Round 1, 2010 Draft (#3 overall)

YEAR	TEAM	LVL	AGE	PA	R	2B	3B	HR	RBI	BB	K	SB	CS	AVG/OBP/SLG
2016	BAL	MLB	23	696	105	40	1	37	96	48	120	0	3	.294/.343/.533
2017	BAL	MLB	24	690	81	33	1	33	95	50	115	9	4	.259/.310/.471
2018	BAL	MLB	25	413	48	21	1	24	65	45	51	8	1	.315/.387/.575
2018	LAN	MLB	25	296	36	14	2	13	42	25	53	6	1	.273/.338/.487
2019	SDN	MLB	26	636	84	34	2	27	89	60	103	10	3	.277/.348/.487

Breakout: 2% Improve: 59% Collapse: 3% Attrition: 6% MLB: 100%
Comparables: Nomar Garciaparra, Cal Ripken Jr., Troy Tulowitzki

You either die the hero or you live long enough to become the villain. Machado was shipped west at the deadline, as a homegrown hero for Orioles fans. Sure, there were a few hiccups along the way, but ultimately memories of a .283/.335/.487 line with 162 homers and breathtaking, highlight-reel defense will always be associated with Machado's time on the left side at Camden Yards. If you go by the stat line, his stint in the City of Angels was pretty good, if not quite vintage Machado. But then the playoffs arrived, and along with them came overly aggressive slides (to be charitable), comments defending the lollygaggers of the world and a swing so long its Blu-ray required two discs. The truth is, everybody loves a villain. Whether it's the Joker, Hannibal Lecter or Marty Scurll, every great heel eventually turns babyface. Is Machado really a baseball villain? Time will tell. Is Machado a generational talent, halfway to Ernie Banks' career WARP by the age of 26? Yes, yes he is.

YEAR	TEAM	LVL	AGE	PA	DRC+	VORP	BABIP	BRR	FRAA	WARP
2016	BAL	MLB	23	696	131	46.7	.309	0.0	3B(114): 8.6, SS(45): -0.5	6.2
2017	BAL	MLB	24	690	106	19.5	.265	-4.1	3B(156): -6.2	2.0
2018	BAL	MLB	25	413	141	40.8	.311	-0.5	SS(96): -4.5	3.5
2018	LAN	MLB	25	296	142	21.2	.296	1.4	SS(51): -4.5, 3B(16): 3.1	2.8
2019	SDN	MLB	26	636	123	33.3	.294	-0.1	3B 3	3.7

Manny Machado, continued

Batted Ball Distribution

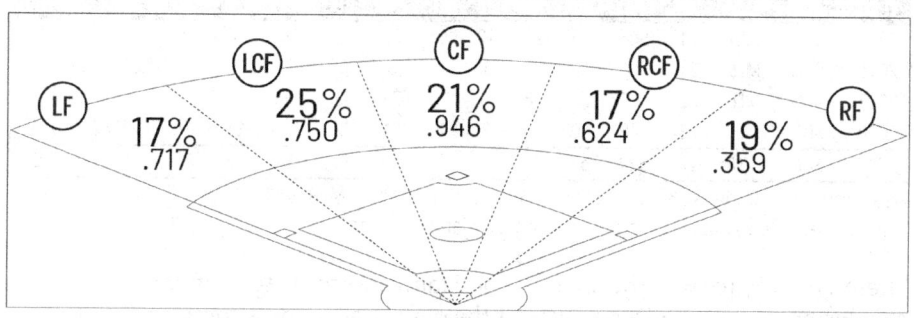

Strike Zone vs LHP   *Strike Zone vs RHP*

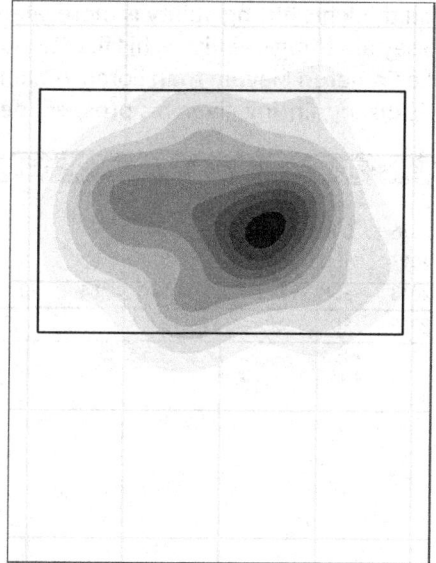

Manuel Margot CF

Born: 09/28/94 Age: 24 Bats: R Throws: R
Height: 5'11" Weight: 180 Origin: International Free Agent, 2011

YEAR	TEAM	LVL	AGE	PA	R	2B	3B	HR	RBI	BB	K	SB	CS	AVG/OBP/SLG
2016	ELP	AAA	21	566	98	21	12	6	55	36	64	30	11	.304/.351/.426
2016	SDN	MLB	21	37	4	4	1	0	3	0	7	2	0	.243/.243/.405
2017	SDN	MLB	22	529	53	18	7	13	39	35	106	17	7	.263/.313/.409
2018	SDN	MLB	23	519	50	26	8	8	51	32	88	11	10	.245/.292/.384
2019	SDN	MLB	24	524	67	21	6	11	48	36	91	16	8	.255/.310/.392

Breakout: 12% Improve: 56% Collapse: 6% Attrition: 6% MLB: 95%
Comparables: Melky Cabrera, Lastings Milledge, Alejandro De Aza

There's no way to twist the splits in good faith and come to a different conclusion: Margot had a bad year at the plate. Following a competent but unspectacular rookie season, his offensive regression was arguably the worst development of the year for the Friars. He's still as athletic and rangy in the outfield as ever and he'll put a charge into the ball just often enough to make you think his hitting ability is more latent than dormant. But while it's too early to say anything definitive, his first 1,000 plate appearances suggest he's more like Cameron Maybin than Lorenzo Cain. That's not the end of the world, even if it is disappointing given his prospect pedigree.

YEAR	TEAM	LVL	AGE	PA	DRC+	VORP	BABIP	BRR	FRAA	WARP
2016	ELP	AAA	21	566	104	30.8	.335	7.9	CF(121): 19.3, RF(1): 0.2	4.0
2016	SDN	MLB	21	37	71	2.4	.300	0.8	CF(9): 0.6, RF(1): 0.1	0.1
2017	SDN	MLB	22	529	90	23.6	.309	1.3	CF(123): -1.0	1.2
2018	SDN	MLB	23	519	84	10.1	.281	0.9	CF(136): -4.9	0.4
2019	SDN	MLB	24	524	87	13.9	.289	0.7	CF 1	1.3

Manuel Margot, continued

Batted Ball Distribution

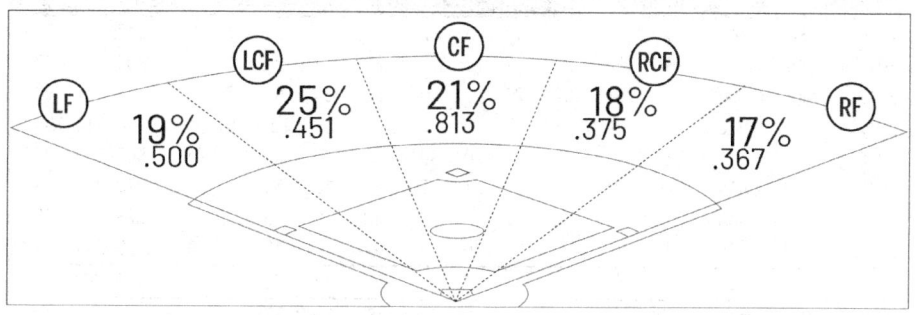

Strike Zone vs LHP   Strike Zone vs RHP

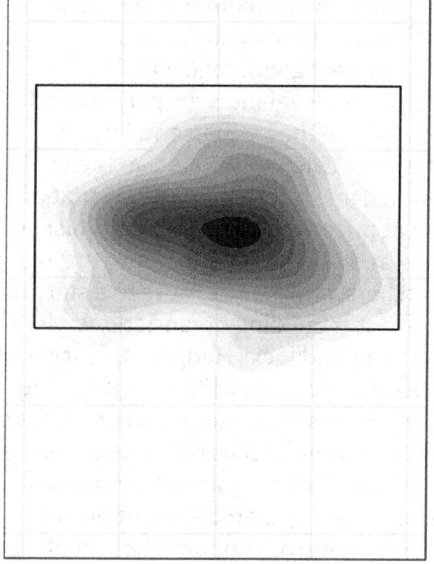

Francisco Mejia   C

Born: 10/27/95   Age: 23   Bats: B   Throws: R
Height: 5'10"   Weight: 180   Origin: International Free Agent, 2012

YEAR	TEAM	LVL	AGE	PA	R	2B	3B	HR	RBI	BB	K	SB	CS	AVG/OBP/SLG
2016	LKC	A	20	259	41	17	3	7	51	15	39	1	0	.347/.384/.531
2016	LYN	A+	20	184	22	12	1	4	29	13	24	1	2	.333/.380/.488
2017	AKR	AA	21	383	52	21	2	14	52	24	53	7	2	.297/.346/.490
2017	CLE	MLB	21	14	1	0	0	0	1	1	3	0	0	.154/.214/.154
2018	CLE	MLB	22	4	0	0	0	0	0	2	0	0	0	.000/.500/.000
2018	COH	AAA	22	336	32	22	1	7	45	18	58	0	0	.279/.328/.426
2018	ELP	AAA	22	132	22	8	1	7	23	7	25	0	0	.328/.364/.582
2018	SDN	MLB	22	58	6	2	0	3	8	3	19	0	0	.185/.241/.389
2019	SDN	MLB	23	300	30	15	1	10	36	15	62	1	0	.240/.284/.409

Breakout: 19%   Improve: 47%   Collapse: 2%   Attrition: 21%   MLB: 57%
Comparables: Hank Conger, Travis d'Arnaud, Jeff Mathis

YEAR	TEAM	P. COUNT	FRM RUNS	BLK RUNS	THRW RUNS	TOT RUNS
2017	AKR	9761	-0.5	-0.8	-0.1	0.7
2017	CLE	40	0.0	0.0	0.0	3.2
2018	COH	5559	2.6	0.7	0.3	3.8
2018	ELP	3547	0.0	0.0	0.2	0.6
2018	SDN	1484	-0.7	-0.8	0.0	-0.7
2019	SDN	8282	-2.8	-0.8	-0.4	-4.0

You don't often see trades like this anymore: A premium prospect at a critical position dealt for two (admittedly good) relievers. But between Cleveland's desperate need to reshape the bullpen and Mejia's desire to catch full-time, San Diego landed an enticing young player at a great price. With Austin Hedges also in tow and Austin Allen charging through the minors, the Padres are flush with catchers, and Mejia's route to a starting job isn't quite as obvious as it would be in most rebuilding organizations. His arm is top-notch, but he's just an okay receiver and lacks Hedges' defensive chops; a shift down the defensive spectrum is a possibility. He'll have to hit regardless of where he plays, and despite less-than-sterling pitch selection skills, the consensus is that he will: He's a potential plus hitter who has the pop to blast 20+ homers annually at maturity. He's very adept at making contact, and he's hit at every minor league stop. Like any hit tool-reliant player though, it's hard to feel comfortable calling him a lineup anchor until he actually performs. As a prospect, Mejia is practically the first name below the "can't miss" tier.

YEAR	TEAM	LVL	AGE	PA	DRC+	VORP	BABIP	BRR	FRAA	WARP
2016	LKC	A	20	259	159	29.7	.388	2.3	C(52): 1.5	2.8
2016	LYN	A+	20	184	143	16.8	.366	-0.1	C(35): 0.6	1.1
2017	AKR	AA	21	383	131	32.5	.311	1.5	C(72): 1.6, 3B(1): -0.1	2.4
2017	CLE	MLB	21	14	78	-1.7	.200	-0.3	C(3): 0.0	0.0
2018	CLE	MLB	22	4	69	0.1	.000	0.0		0.0
2018	COH	AAA	22	336	101	9.4	.321	-1.2	C(41): 4.6, LF(22): -3.2	0.7
2018	ELP	AAA	22	132	122	11.8	.359	0.7	C(26): 1.3	0.9
2018	SDN	MLB	22	58	73	-0.3	.219	0.2	C(10): -1.7	-0.1
2019	SDN	MLB	23	300	80	5.7	.273	-0.5	C -4	0.0

San Diego Padres 2019

Francisco Mejia, continued

Batted Ball Distribution

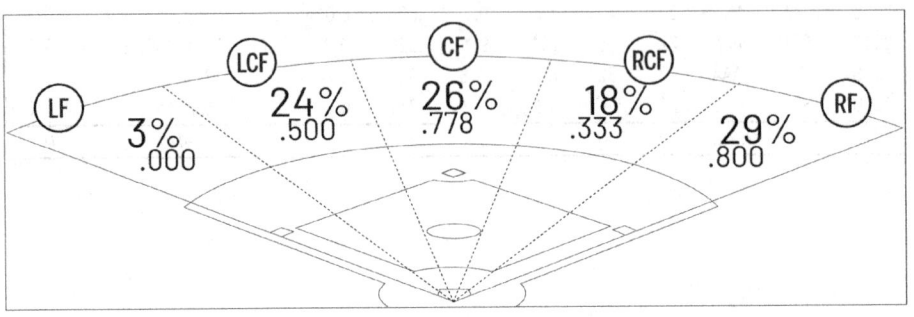

Strike Zone vs LHP   **Strike Zone vs RHP**

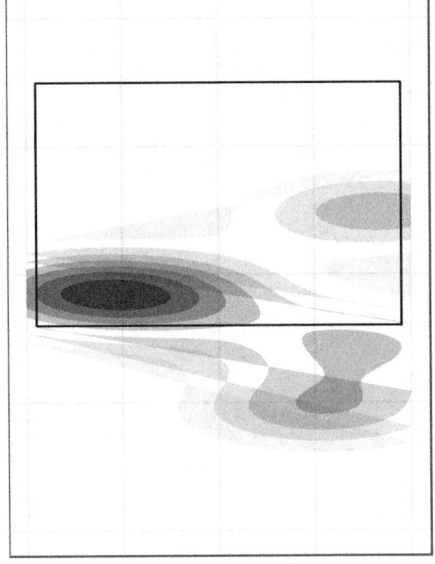

Wil Myers LF

Born: 12/10/90 Age: 28 Bats: R Throws: R
Height: 6'3" Weight: 205 Origin: Round 3, 2009 Draft (#91 overall)

YEAR	TEAM	LVL	AGE	PA	R	2B	3B	HR	RBI	BB	K	SB	CS	AVG/OBP/SLG
2016	SDN	MLB	25	676	99	29	4	28	94	68	160	28	6	.259/.336/.461
2017	SDN	MLB	26	649	80	29	3	30	74	70	180	20	6	.243/.328/.464
2018	SDN	MLB	27	343	39	25	1	11	39	30	94	13	1	.253/.318/.446
2019	SDN	MLB	28	578	84	26	2	20	63	61	147	21	5	.244/.328/.420

Breakout: 7% Improve: 45% Collapse: 14% Attrition: 7% MLB: 98%
Comparables: Dave Hollins, Jhonny Peralta, Morgan Ensberg

It's one thing for a top prospect to bust. To have talent and hope and potential and still fall short may be difficult to swallow, but it's also common and understandable. We all know at least one of those folks from high school. Far more perplexing are the blue chippers who turn into Phil Hughes or Jay Bruce. Back in 2016, when he made the All-Star team and hit .286/.351/.522 in the first half, Myers looked like he was finally developing into the star we'd long expected. But after a second-half slump and two years of solid but hardly special production, it increasingly appears that he's more of a good player than a building block. That the Padres have asked him to switch positions for the fifth time this decade—third base on your bingo cards, folks—all but confirms as much. Perhaps it's the lingering hype from his time as one of baseball's top prospects, or the notoriety that surrounded him throughout the endless litigation of the James Shields trade, but that feels like a bit of a letdown. That's not necessarily fair, but neither was expecting your Ivy League buddy to cure cancer.

YEAR	TEAM	LVL	AGE	PA	DRC+	VORP	BABIP	BRR	FRAA	WARP
2016	SDN	MLB	25	676	108	33.2	.305	5.2	1B(149): 1.8, RF(7): -0.3	2.2
2017	SDN	MLB	26	649	108	28.7	.297	1.1	1B(154): -1.8	1.4
2018	SDN	MLB	27	343	91	14.4	.327	1.3	3B(36): -4.3, LF(31): 0.8	0.6
2019	SDN	MLB	28	578	104	21.8	.302	2.3	LF 2, 1B 0	2.4

Wil Myers, continued

Batted Ball Distribution

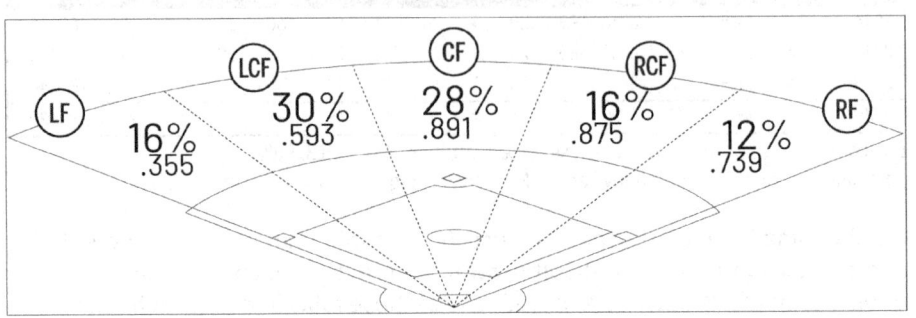

Strike Zone vs LHP   **Strike Zone vs RHP**

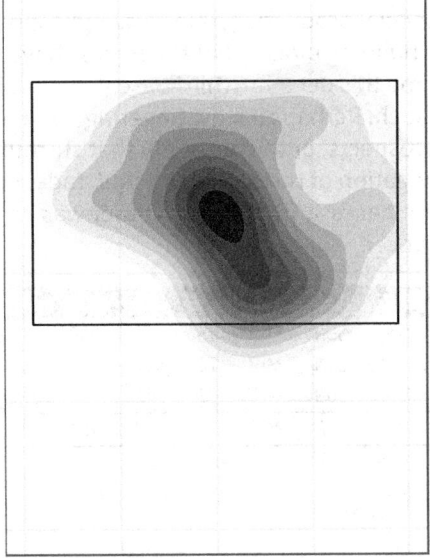

Jose Pirela 2B

Born: 11/21/89 Age: 29 Bats: R Throws: R
Height: 6'0" Weight: 220 Origin: Undrafted Free Agent, 2006

YEAR	TEAM	LVL	AGE	PA	R	2B	3B	HR	RBI	BB	K	SB	CS	AVG/OBP/SLG
2016	SDN	MLB	26	41	2	2	0	0	0	1	9	0	1	.154/.175/.205
2016	ELP	AAA	26	146	19	7	3	2	16	9	21	1	1	.248/.295/.387
2017	ELP	AAA	27	201	37	10	3	13	42	15	26	8	3	.331/.387/.635
2017	SDN	MLB	27	344	43	25	4	10	40	27	71	4	3	.288/.347/.490
2018	SDN	MLB	28	473	54	23	2	5	32	30	89	6	3	.249/.300/.345
2019	SDN	MLB	29	117	12	5	1	3	13	8	23	2	1	.243/.299/.393

Breakout: 10% Improve: 34% Collapse: 11% Attrition: 24% MLB: 72%
Comparables: Whit Merrifield, Ramiro Pena, Russ Adams

Pirela was one of the earliest fringe prospects to land in San Diego following the club's decision to rebuild. After hitting well in limited action back in 2017, he cratered last year, losing more than 150 points off his slugging percentage; by year's end, he'd fallen out of the lineup. In hindsight, his 2017 power surge almost certainly said more about the worst excesses of the juiced ball than about Pirela himself. Regardless, entering his age-29 season and coming off a replacement-level campaign, it appears that Pirela has missed his best chance to establish himself on the roster.

YEAR	TEAM	LVL	AGE	PA	DRC+	VORP	BABIP	BRR	FRAA	WARP
2016	SDN	MLB	26	41	59	-3.9	.200	-0.7	2B(12): -1.5, RF(1): 0.0	-0.3
2016	ELP	AAA	26	146	69	-4.2	.281	0.4	LF(17): -0.9, RF(8): -0.7	-0.5
2017	ELP	AAA	27	201	158	17.5	.329	-1.4	1B(26): 3.1, LF(12): 2.0	1.7
2017	SDN	MLB	27	344	105	22.8	.343	0.3	LF(68): 6.3, 2B(7): -0.1	1.6
2018	SDN	MLB	28	473	72	-5.9	.301	-1.5	2B(77): 0.3, LF(31): -1.3	-0.6
2019	SDN	MLB	29	117	84	1.5	.277	-0.1	2B 0, LF 0	0.1

Jose Pirela, continued

Batted Ball Distribution

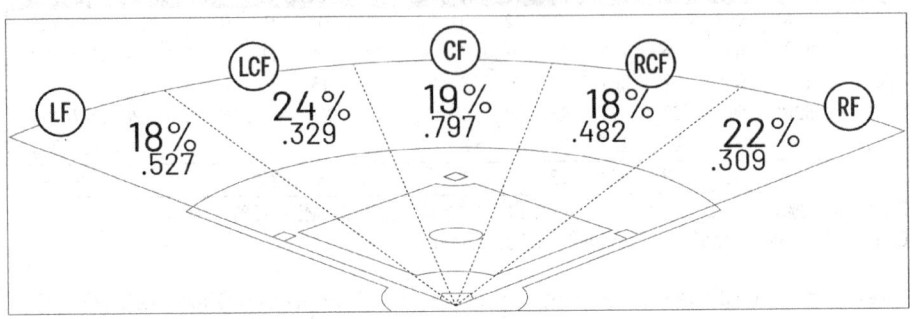

Strike Zone vs LHP　　　**Strike Zone vs RHP**

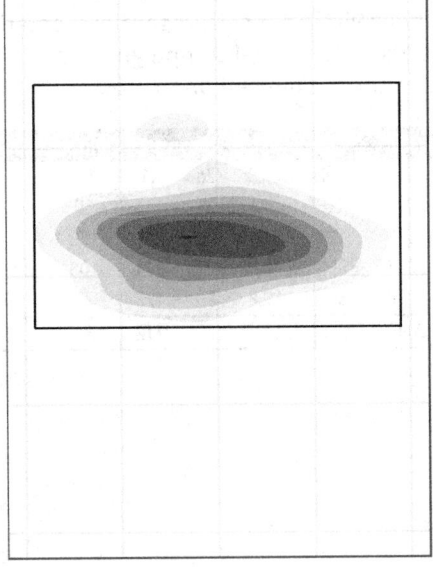

Hunter Renfroe   LF

Born: 01/28/92   Age: 27   Bats: R   Throws: R
Height: 6'1"   Weight: 220   Origin: Round 1, 2013 Draft (#13 overall)

YEAR	TEAM	LVL	AGE	PA	R	2B	3B	HR	RBI	BB	K	SB	CS	AVG/OBP/SLG
2016	ELP	AAA	24	563	95	34	5	30	105	22	115	5	2	.306/.336/.557
2016	SDN	MLB	24	36	8	3	0	4	14	1	5	0	0	.371/.389/.800
2017	ELP	AAA	25	61	18	7	1	4	18	6	7	1	0	.509/.557/.891
2017	SDN	MLB	25	479	51	25	1	26	58	27	140	3	0	.231/.284/.467
2018	ELP	AAA	26	43	6	1	0	2	4	2	10	0	0	.220/.256/.390
2018	SDN	MLB	26	441	53	23	1	26	68	30	109	2	1	.248/.302/.504
2019	SDN	MLB	27	443	53	22	2	20	63	28	110	2	1	.248/.302/.458

Breakout: 10%   Improve: 48%   Collapse: 12%   Attrition: 11%   MLB: 89%
Comparables: Mark Trumbo, Corey Dickerson, J.D. Martinez

It took a long time for Renfroe—who was considered an advanced college bat when the Padres drafted him back in 2013—to establish himself as a big-leaguer. Throughout his minor league career and first season in San Diego, Renfroe's undisciplined hacking threatened to undercut prodigious in-game power. But while he's never going to win a batting title or post a great walk rate, he's managed to sand down the roughest edges in his game, fine-tuning his approach just enough to make everything work. The .248/.302/.504 slash line he posted last year seems like a reasonable approximation of his talent going forward. There will be slumps but also 480-foot homers, and enough of the latter to justify his spot in the middle of the order. He's like a recent grad who finally found a reliable job after a few false starts: You knew he had the talent, it took a long time to get here, you're not entirely sure he'll show up to work every day, but he's definitely in a better place now than six months ago.

YEAR	TEAM	LVL	AGE	PA	DRC+	VORP	BABIP	BRR	FRAA	WARP
2016	ELP	AAA	24	563	122	22.2	.339	1.8	RF(111): 5.8, CF(12): -0.9	2.2
2016	SDN	MLB	24	36	118	6.1	.346	0.2	RF(9): 0.7	0.2
2017	ELP	AAA	25	61	249	16.8	.545	0.8	RF(12): 1.9	1.3
2017	SDN	MLB	25	479	94	16.0	.275	-0.9	RF(120): -2.1	0.4
2018	ELP	AAA	26	43	73	-0.8	.241	-0.1	RF(9): 2.4	0.1
2018	SDN	MLB	26	441	110	18.4	.271	-1.2	LF(58): -1.3, RF(50): 6.6	2.0
2019	SDN	MLB	27	443	104	14.6	.287	-0.5	RF 1, LF 0	1.5

Hunter Renfroe, continued

Batted Ball Distribution

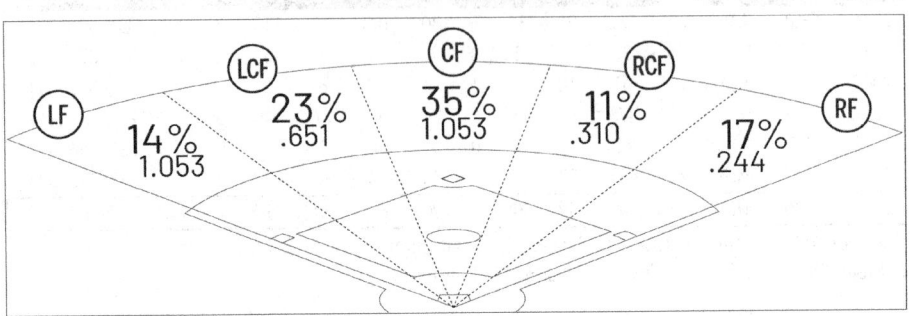

LF	LCF	CF	RCF	RF
14%	23%	35%	11%	17%
1.053	.651	1.053	.310	.244

Strike Zone vs LHP   **Strike Zone vs RHP**

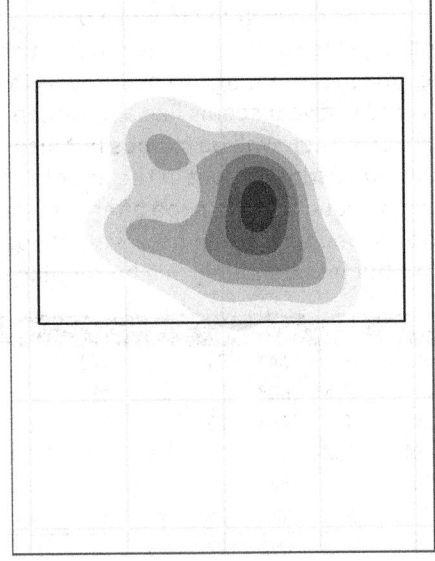

Franmil Reyes RF

Born: 07/07/95 Age: 23 Bats: R Throws: R
Height: 6'5" Weight: 275 Origin: International Free Agent, 2011

YEAR	TEAM	LVL	AGE	PA	R	2B	3B	HR	RBI	BB	K	SB	CS	AVG/OBP/SLG
2016	LEL	A+	20	547	63	32	3	16	83	47	108	2	3	.278/.340/.452
2017	SAN	AA	21	566	79	27	1	25	102	48	134	4	4	.258/.322/.464
2018	ELP	AAA	22	250	50	11	1	16	52	37	59	0	0	.324/.428/.614
2018	SDN	MLB	22	285	36	9	0	16	31	24	80	0	0	.280/.340/.498
2019	SDN	MLB	23	374	48	14	1	18	55	39	100	0	0	.255/.338/.468

Breakout: 10% Improve: 36% Collapse: 7% Attrition: 17% MLB: 66%
Comparables: Jorge Soler, Wil Myers, Domonic Brown

Hey look, another a power-hitting corner outfielder with strikeout issues and a shaky glove! It's a fairly common prototype in this organization, and as a profile, it's generally a bit of a tease; in many cases, plus (or plus-plus) power is the only carrying tool here and you're just sorta hoping the guy turns into Adam Duvall. Once in a while though, there's a bit more bat to go with that power, and the question is whether Reyes's torrid finish indicates that he's become one of those special cases.

After struggling and striking out in nearly 40 percent of his plate appearances in his first 40 big league games, Reyes caught fire over the last two months of the season. He hit .318/.385/.548 down the stretch, with shockingly acceptable walk and strikeout rates and a handful of monster home runs. His career trajectory and minor league body of work suggests he was just running hot, but he suddenly stopped missing fastballs in August and if that holds true, pitchers have an adjustment to make. Reyes's career could go in a lot of directions from here, depending on how he adjusts to the adjustments, but regardless, he's emerged as a real part of the team's present. On a long list of compelling Padres to follow in 2019, he's near the top of the heap.

YEAR	TEAM	LVL	AGE	PA	DRC+	VORP	BABIP	BRR	FRAA	WARP
2016	LEL	A+	20	547	123	23.2	.324	-0.2	RF(112): 17.3, LF(1): -0.1	2.7
2017	SAN	AA	21	566	117	25.5	.298	-1.1	RF(89): 3.2	0.8
2018	ELP	AAA	22	250	166	20.3	.382	1.9	RF(46): -2.2	2.0
2018	SDN	MLB	22	285	112	14.5	.345	0.3	RF(75): -7.1	0.3
2019	SDN	MLB	23	374	116	18.7	.311	-0.7	RF -1	1.6

San Diego Padres 2019

Franmil Reyes, continued

Batted Ball Distribution

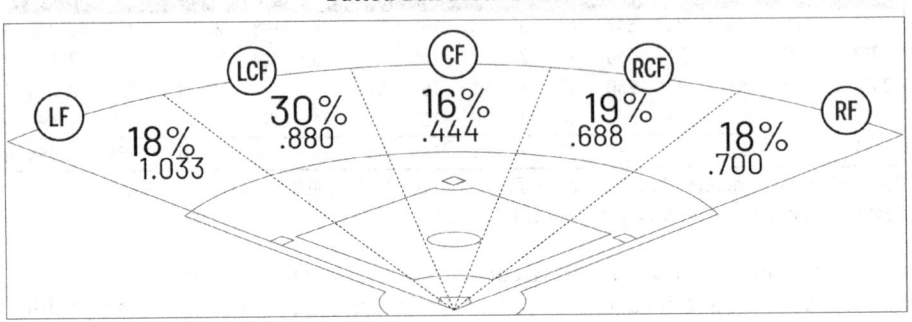

Strike Zone vs LHP   **Strike Zone vs RHP**

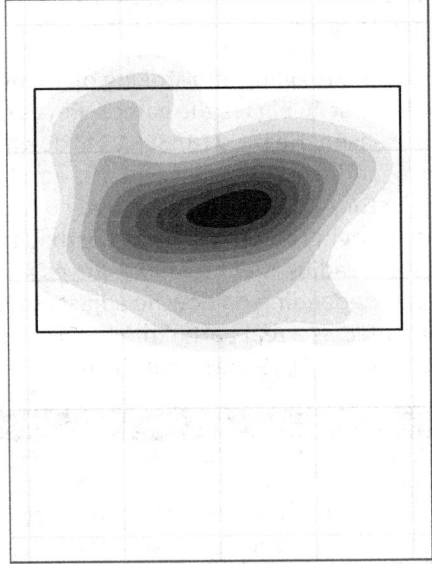

Jose Castillo LHP
Born: 01/10/96   Age: 23   Bats: L   Throws: L
Height: 6'5"   Weight: 246   Origin: International Free Agent, 2012

YEAR	TEAM	LVL	AGE	W	L	SV	G	GS	IP	H	HR	BB/9	K/9	K	GB%	BABIP
2016	FTW	A	20	1	1	1	9	0	23^2	23	0	1.5	13.3	35	47%	.397
2016	LEL	A+	20	1	0	0	7	0	11^1	15	1	4.0	5.6	7	51%	.368
2017	LEL	A+	21	3	2	1	39	0	47	38	0	4.2	9.4	49	42%	.297
2017	SAN	AA	21	1	0	0	8	0	9^1	8	1	3.9	9.6	10	28%	.292
2018	SAN	AA	22	2	1	5	12	0	15	14	0	4.8	15.6	26	38%	.438
2018	ELP	AAA	22	1	0	3	10	0	11^1	6	1	1.6	10.3	13	43%	.185
2018	SDN	MLB	22	3	3	0	37	0	38^1	23	3	2.8	12.2	52	39%	.250
2019	SDN	MLB	23	2	1	0	30	0	31^2	27	4	4.4	10.9	38	40%	.298

Breakout: 14%   Improve: 22%   Collapse: 19%   Attrition: 27%   MLB: 47%
Comparables: Zach Braddock, Jose Alvarado, Jon Meloan

It's been a long six years since Castillo signed the fourth-largest J2 deal of the 2012 class. In that time, he's lost the velocity that initially excited scouts, got traded from Tampa Bay to San Diego, moved to the bullpen, re-discovered some of that missing gas, and made his major league debut. Along the way, he's thoughtfully and candidly spoke about the difficulties that Latin American kids have leaving home and living in an entirely different culture as a teenager. Castillo is one to root for, and given that his fastball-slider combination is electric enough to miss plenty of bats, you'll presumably have several years to do so.

YEAR	TEAM	LVL	AGE	WHIP	ERA	DRA	WARP	MPH	FB%	WHF	CSP
2016	FTW	A	20	1.14	2.28	2.36	0.7				
2016	LEL	A+	20	1.76	1.59	4.70	0.0				
2017	LEL	A+	21	1.28	2.87	5.24	-0.2				
2017	SAN	AA	21	1.29	2.89	2.57	0.2				
2018	SAN	AA	22	1.47	3.00	2.17	0.5				
2018	ELP	AAA	22	0.71	0.79	3.33	0.2				
2018	SDN	MLB	22	0.91	3.29	3.02	0.8	97.1	55.2	15.5	48.7
2019	SDN	MLB	23	1.34	3.69	4.03	0.3	97.0	57.2	16.1	50.4

San Diego Padres 2019

Jose Castillo, continued

Pitch Shape vs LHH

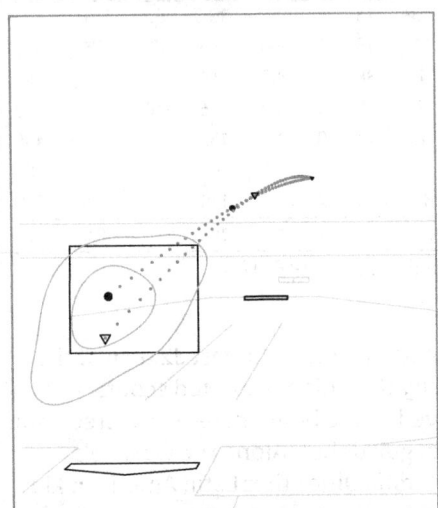

Pitch Shape vs RHH

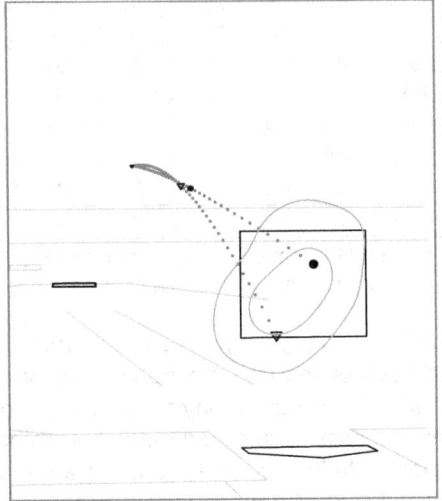

Type	Frequency	Velocity	H Movement	V Movement
● Fastball	55.2%	95.4 [109]	6.6 [100]	-13.7 [107]
☐ Sinker				
+ Cutter				
▲ Changeup	0.2%	89.1 [115]	11.3 [100]	-21.6 [117]
✕ Splitter				
▽ Slider	44.6%	83.9 [98]	-6.5 [107]	-35.6 [92]
◇ Curveball				
⊕ Slow Curveball				
✳ Knuckleball				
▼ Screwball				

46 - Padres Player Analysis

Miguel Diaz RHP

Born: 11/28/94   Age: 24   Bats: R   Throws: R
Height: 6'0"   Weight: 214   Origin: International Free Agent, 2011

YEAR	TEAM	LVL	AGE	W	L	SV	G	GS	IP	H	HR	BB/9	K/9	K	GB%	BABIP
2016	WIS	A	21	1	8	3	26	15	94^2	83	7	2.8	8.7	91	47%	.279
2017	SDN	MLB	22	1	1	0	31	3	41^2	44	11	5.4	7.1	33	41%	.275
2018	ELP	AAA	23	0	3	0	5	2	13^1	17	2	8.8	10.1	15	40%	.375
2018	SAN	AA	23	5	2	2	19	9	65	45	4	4.2	9.1	66	57%	.253
2018	SDN	MLB	23	1	0	0	11	0	18^2	16	2	5.8	14.5	30	35%	.341
2019	*SDN*	*MLB*	*24*	*2*	*3*	*0*	*23*	*5*	*44*	*41*	*5*	*4.6*	*8.8*	*43*	*44%*	*.295*

Breakout: 24%   Improve: 32%   Collapse: 12%   Attrition: 20%   MLB: 54%
Comparables: Chris Ray, Keynan Middleton, Ian Krol

Diaz struck out more than a third of the batters he faced last year, which makes him about the 11th most exciting arm in San Diego's absurdly deep relief corps. He can reach the mid-90s without breaking a sweat and he's the rare reliever who misses bats with three distinct offerings. The problem is that he has no clue where any of them are going. While he doesn't employ the kind of grunting, full-effort, high-octane delivery we normally associate with control issues, his herky-jerk motion is very difficult to repeat and he's always struggled to throw strikes. There's enough arm strength here for him to keep getting chances, but given the Padres' bullpen depth, he'll have to make the most of them soon.

YEAR	TEAM	LVL	AGE	WHIP	ERA	DRA	WARP	MPH	FB%	WHF	CSP
2016	WIS	A	21	1.18	3.71	3.47	1.6				
2017	SDN	MLB	22	1.66	7.34	7.15	-0.9	97.6	65.5	9.3	47.1
2018	ELP	AAA	23	2.25	8.10	4.74	0.1				
2018	SAN	AA	23	1.15	2.35	3.73	1.1				
2018	SDN	MLB	23	1.50	4.82	3.24	0.4	97.4	55.3	17.9	45.5
2019	*SDN*	*MLB*	*24*	*1.45*	*4.45*	*4.69*	*0.1*	*97.3*	*63.7*	*12.7*	*47.6*

San Diego Padres 2019

Miguel Diaz, continued

Pitch Shape vs LHH

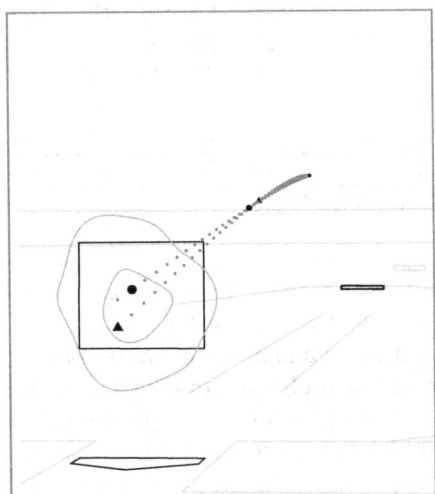

Pitch Shape vs RHH

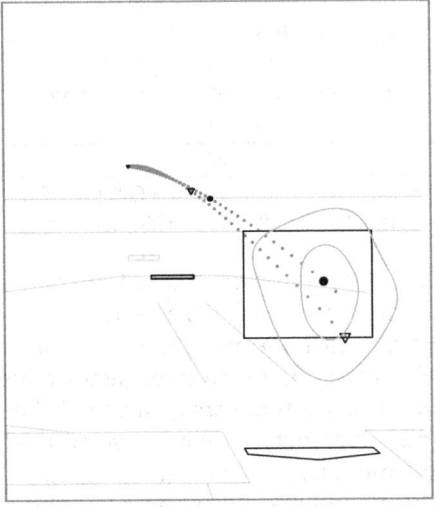

Type	Frequency	Velocity	H Movement	V Movement
● Fastball	53.0%	96 [111]	-8.6 [91]	-12.9 [109]
☐ Sinker	2.3%	94.7 [111]	-12.5 [101]	-18 [108]
+ Cutter				
▲ Changeup	19.6%	87.8 [110]	-12.1 [96]	-26.6 [102]
✕ Splitter				
▽ Slider	25.1%	84.9 [102]	6.2 [106]	-33.5 [99]
◇ Curveball				
⊕ Slow Curveball				
✳ Knuckleball				
▼ Screwball				

Robbie Erlin   LHP

Born: 10/08/90   Age: 28   Bats: R   Throws: L
Height: 6'0"   Weight: 190   Origin: Round 3, 2009 Draft (#93 overall)

YEAR	TEAM	LVL	AGE	W	L	SV	G	GS	IP	H	HR	BB/9	K/9	K	GB%	BABIP
2016	SDN	MLB	25	1	2	0	3	2	15^2	12	3	1.7	7.5	13	43%	.231
2018	SDN	MLB	27	4	7	0	39	12	109	112	12	1.0	7.3	88	48%	.306
2019	*SDN*	*MLB*	*28*	*7*	*8*	*0*	*43*	*19*	*120*	*126*	*18*	*2.9*	*7.8*	*105*	*45%*	*.302*

Breakout: 16%   Improve: 45%   Collapse: 17%   Attrition: 19%   MLB: 93%
Comparables: Doug Fister, Anthony DeSclafani, Liam Hendriks

Coming up through the minors, Erlin universally earned praise as a smart and polished, if unspectacular, starter. He was the safest kind of arm, a low-effort pitchability southpaw who could spin a curve and keep hitters off balance with his changeup. But the Volvo of pitching prospects has been anything but reliable as a big leaguer. Now 28, Erlin has battled various ailments over the last four years, most seriously a torn UCL that cost him most of 2016 and all of 2017.

Just when he looked like the afterthought of the 40-man roster, Erlin turned in a sneaky good campaign last year, leading the rotation in DRA and all Padres pitchers in WARP. Befitting his reputation as a control pitcher, he walked only 12 hitters across 100 innings while generating far more grounders than flies. Strikes and weak contact have always been a winning combination and by years end, he'd bounced from long relief into the starting five. A stable slot in the back of a rotation has long seemed like Erlin's destiny, and with good health, he may finally fulfill it in 2019.

YEAR	TEAM	LVL	AGE	WHIP	ERA	DRA	WARP	MPH	FB%	WHF	CSP
2016	SDN	MLB	25	0.96	4.02	4.10	0.2	91.4	54.4	9.8	48.2
2018	SDN	MLB	27	1.14	4.21	3.05	2.6	91.8	59.2	10.3	52
2019	*SDN*	*MLB*	*28*	*1.38*	*4.40*	*4.67*	*0.5*	*91.2*	*59.2*	*10.3*	*50.9*

Robbie Erlin, continued

Pitch Shape vs LHH

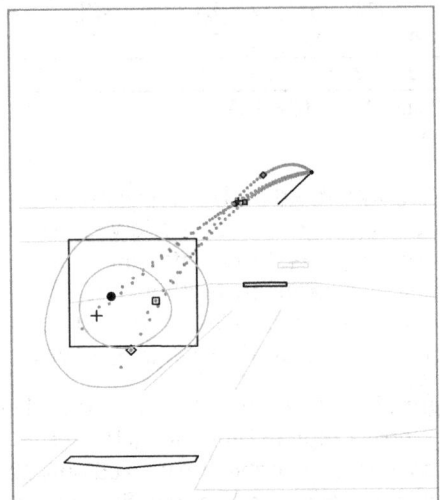

Pitch Shape vs RHH

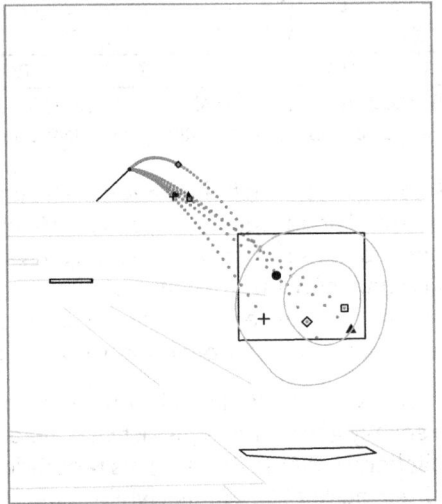

Type	Frequency	Velocity	H Movement	V Movement
● Fastball	31.3%	91 [95]	5.8 [104]	-14.2 [105]
☐ Sinker	27.9%	90.9 [92]	12.2 [104]	-18 [108]
+ Cutter	4.8%	88.4 [98]	-0.5 [92]	-22.8 [104]
▲ Changeup	16.5%	84.8 [98]	7.8 [118]	-24.6 [108]
✕ Splitter				
▽ Slider	1.0%	84.4 [100]	-1.5 [86]	-32.3 [102]
◇ Curveball	18.6%	76.9 [94]	-1.5 [73]	-55 [84]
⊕ Slow Curveball				
✳ Knuckleball				
▼ Screwball				

Brett Kennedy   RHP

Born: 08/04/94   Age: 24   Bats: R   Throws: R
Height: 6'0"   Weight: 200   Origin: Round 11, 2015 Draft (#327 overall)

YEAR	TEAM	LVL	AGE	W	L	SV	G	GS	IP	H	HR	BB/9	K/9	K	GB%	BABIP
2016	FTW	A	21	2	1	0	6	6	28^1	29	2	2.2	12.1	38	54%	.391
2016	LEL	A+	21	6	10	0	22	22	113^2	114	9	3.5	8.6	109	48%	.325
2017	SAN	AA	22	13	7	0	26	26	141	133	16	2.4	8.6	134	41%	.298
2018	ELP	AAA	23	10	0	0	16	16	89^1	77	6	2.3	8.1	80	54%	.285
2018	SDN	MLB	23	1	2	0	6	6	26^2	36	6	4.1	6.1	18	43%	.333
2019	SDN	MLB	24	5	5	0	46	10	88	87	11	3.6	8.0	78	45%	.298

Breakout: 11%   Improve: 20%   Collapse: 9%   Attrition: 24%   MLB: 41%
Comparables: Ricardo Pinto, David Phelps, J.R. Graham

We've reached the point in baseball's history where a righty throwing 92 mph with two functional secondaries isn't a potential No. 3 or 4 starter, but instead nearly an afterthought on top prospect lists, like the jar of Cheerios at a continental breakfast. Kennedy has actually done pretty well to make it this far, rising from 11th-round obscurity to the big leagues in only three seasons. The rookie out of Fordham is a bulldog on the mound, and he brings plenty of moxie and pretty good command out to the hill. Whether that's sufficient is for the fates to sort out, but his chances were better 10 years ago.

YEAR	TEAM	LVL	AGE	WHIP	ERA	DRA	WARP	MPH	FB%	WHF	CSP
2016	FTW	A	21	1.27	2.54	2.90	0.7				
2016	LEL	A+	21	1.39	3.80	3.88	2.1				
2017	SAN	AA	22	1.21	3.70	4.07	1.8				
2018	ELP	AAA	23	1.12	2.72	4.09	1.5				
2018	SDN	MLB	23	1.80	6.75	6.98	-0.5	94.4	67.6	9.3	44.6
2019	SDN	MLB	24	1.39	4.36	4.61	0.3	94.2	69.6	9.6	46

San Diego Padres 2019

Brett Kennedy, continued

Pitch Shape vs LHH

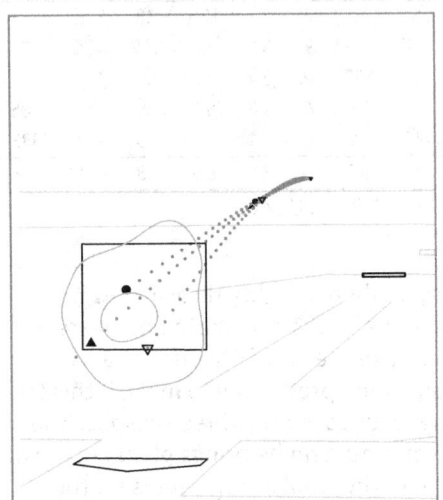

Pitch Shape vs RHH

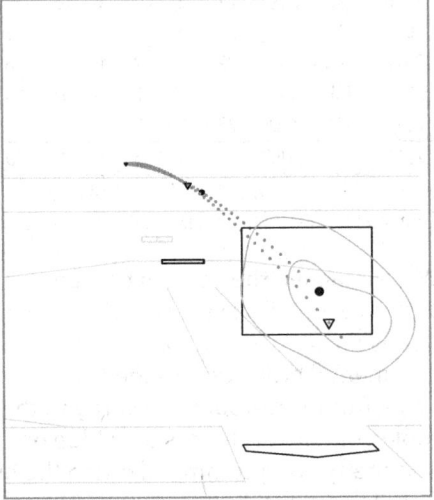

Type	Frequency	Velocity	H Movement	V Movement
● Fastball	67.6%	92.1 [99]	-10.3 [83]	-17.7 [94]
☐ Sinker				
+ Cutter				
▲ Changeup	8.3%	83.5 [93]	-9.9 [107]	-26 [104]
× Splitter				
▽ Slider	22.7%	83.1 [94]	0 [79]	-32.3 [102]
◇ Curveball	1.4%	78.8 [101]	1.6 [74]	-41.1 [116]
⊕ Slow Curveball				
✳ Knuckleball				
▼ Screwball				

Eric Lauer LHP

Born: 06/03/95   Age: 24   Bats: R   Throws: L
Height: 6'3"   Weight: 205   Origin: Round 1, 2016 Draft (#25 overall)

YEAR	TEAM	LVL	AGE	W	L	SV	G	GS	IP	H	HR	BB/9	K/9	K	GB%	BABIP
2016	TRI	A-	21	1	0	0	7	7	25	17	0	2.5	10.1	28	52%	.279
2017	LEL	A+	22	2	5	0	12	12	67^2	65	4	2.5	11.2	84	42%	.351
2017	SAN	AA	22	4	3	0	10	9	55	52	6	2.8	7.9	48	38%	.295
2018	ELP	AAA	23	2	1	0	4	4	21^1	13	1	3.8	9.3	22	48%	.226
2018	SDN	MLB	23	6	7	0	23	23	112	127	15	3.7	8.0	100	39%	.332
2019	SDN	MLB	24	8	9	0	26	26	130	128	20	3.7	9.1	131	40%	.298

Breakout: 20%   Improve: 48%   Collapse: 12%   Attrition: 27%   MLB: 81%
Comparables: Jacob Turner, Derek Holland, Ricky Nolasco

Lauer was the second of many rookies to take a turn in San Diego's rotation last year. Over 23 starts, he pitched to his billing as a low-90s lefty with three distinct offspeed pitches and decent control, but nothing to consistently miss bats with. But after a rough May, he was actually pretty good over his final 16 starts, posting a 3.16 ERA and generating more swings and misses with his slider. He played around with his pitch mix throughout the year, incorporating a cutter and changing his grip on the slider, which now moves a bit slower but with more depth. The result is a more well-rounded arsenal that gives hitters a greater variety of looks to stew over. It's hard to be bullish about a guy like this—he still doesn't have a true out pitch—but it's possible that the overall numbers slightly undersell Lauer's chances to hang around as a back-end starter for a few years.

YEAR	TEAM	LVL	AGE	WHIP	ERA	DRA	WARP	MPH	FB%	WHF	CSP
2016	TRI	A-	21	0.96	1.44	2.91	0.7				
2017	LEL	A+	22	1.24	2.79	3.52	1.4				
2017	SAN	AA	22	1.25	3.93	3.31	1.2				
2018	ELP	AAA	23	1.03	2.53	6.31	-0.2				
2018	SDN	MLB	23	1.54	4.34	5.27	0.1	93.6	57.9	9.7	51.5
2019	SDN	MLB	24	1.41	4.46	4.77	0.4	93.4	59.6	10	53.1

Eric Lauer, continued

Pitch Shape vs LHH

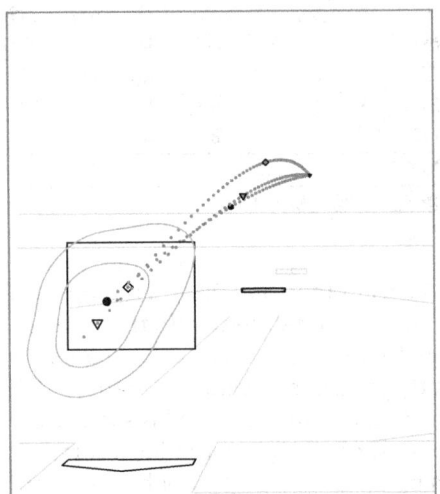

Pitch Shape vs RHH

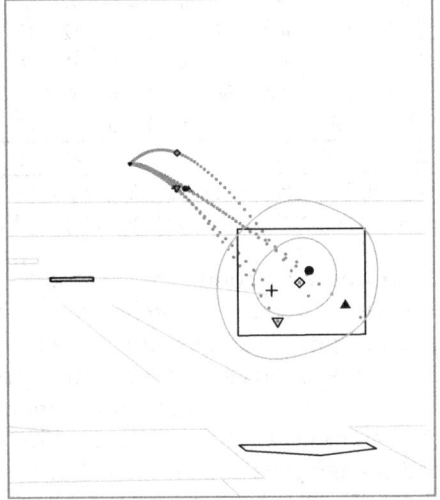

Type	Frequency	Velocity	H Movement	V Movement
● Fastball	57.9%	91.9 [98]	7.9 [94]	-14.2 [105]
☐ Sinker				
+ Cutter	6.5%	90.5 [110]	1.6 [80]	-19.4 [117]
▲ Changeup	3.7%	85.4 [100]	10.4 [105]	-22.3 [115]
✕ Splitter				
▽ Slider	20.3%	86.1 [107]	-1.5 [86]	-28.2 [114]
◇ Curveball	11.7%	75.3 [88]	-3.9 [83]	-50.9 [94]
✥ Slow Curveball				
✳ Knuckleball				
▼ Screwball				

Aaron Loup   LHP

Born: 12/19/87   Age: 31   Bats: L   Throws: L
Height: 5'11"   Weight: 210   Origin: Round 9, 2009 Draft (#280 overall)

YEAR	TEAM	LVL	AGE	W	L	SV	G	GS	IP	H	HR	BB/9	K/9	K	GB%	BABIP
2016	BUF	AAA	28	3	0	1	20	0	19^2	21	0	1.4	11.9	26	54%	.404
2016	TOR	MLB	28	0	0	0	21	0	14^1	15	2	2.5	9.4	15	40%	.342
2017	TOR	MLB	29	2	3	0	70	0	57^2	59	4	4.5	10.0	64	56%	.340
2018	TOR	MLB	30	0	0	0	50	0	35^2	44	4	3.3	10.6	42	50%	.385
2018	PHI	MLB	30	0	0	0	9	0	4	4	0	2.2	4.5	2	69%	.308
2019	SDN	MLB	31	2	2	0	42	0	44	43	5	4.2	9.1	45	49%	.309

Breakout: 28%   Improve: 46%   Collapse: 21%   Attrition: 17%   MLB: 85%
Comparables: Joba Chamberlain, Tyler Yates, Daniel Hudson

It made sense to acquire Loup for their stretch run. The reliable lefty was posting a career-best K rate and inducing more whiffs than ever in his age-30 season, and the Phillies were desperate for someone, *anyone*, to get LHBs out. A forearm strain after two innings of work scuttled those plans, but his run of success with Toronto positions him as a mid-tier first-time free agent. We may not equate Loup with the likes of prime Andrew Miller or Aroldis Chapman or any other member of the elite southpaw relievers for good reason, but a team in search of some left-handed depth that misses out on Miller or Zach Britton in free agency may find Loup to be a worthy consolation prize.

YEAR	TEAM	LVL	AGE	WHIP	ERA	DRA	WARP	MPH	FB%	WHF	CSP
2016	BUF	AAA	28	1.22	1.83	2.62	0.5				
2016	TOR	MLB	28	1.33	5.02	4.76	0.0	94.8	66.7	8.8	52.4
2017	TOR	MLB	29	1.53	3.75	5.68	-0.3	93.7	65.6	10.7	47.1
2018	TOR	MLB	30	1.60	4.54	4.60	0.1	93.7	66.1	12.5	49.6
2018	PHI	MLB	30	1.25	4.50	6.95	-0.1	92.4	66.1	6.8	51.5
2019	SDN	MLB	31	1.46	4.11	4.37	0.2	92.9	65.5	11	49.3

San Diego Padres 2019

Aaron Loup, continued

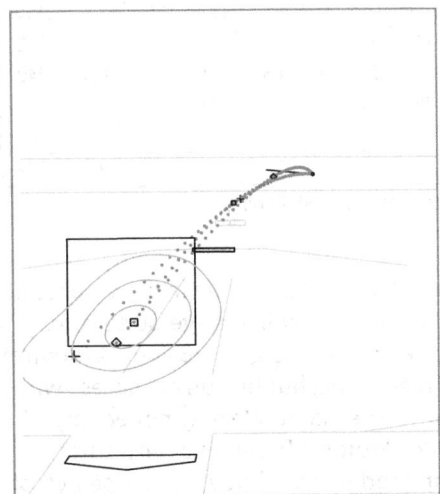

Pitch Shape vs LHH

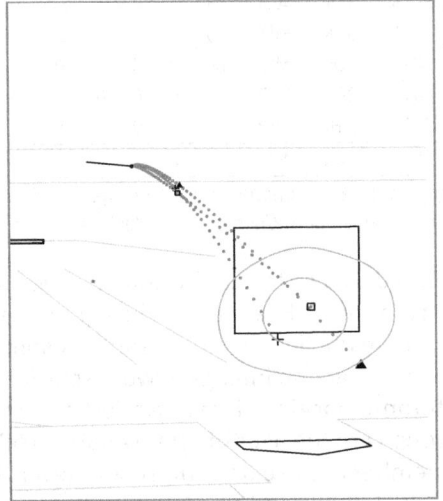

Pitch Shape vs RHH

Type	Frequency	Velocity	H Movement	V Movement
● Fastball				
□ Sinker	65.5%	92.5 [100]	17.6 [59]	-25.1 [84]
+ Cutter	16.3%	84.5 [75]	-0.6 [92]	-33.5 [61]
▲ Changeup	8.6%	80.2 [79]	16.2 [74]	-39.9 [63]
× Splitter				
▽ Slider				
◇ Curveball	9.6%	76.4 [92]	-14.8 [129]	-48.6 [99]
⊕ Slow Curveball				
✳ Knuckleball				
▼ Screwball				

Joey Lucchesi   LHP

Born: 06/06/93   Age: 26   Bats: L   Throws: L
Height: 6'5"   Weight: 204   Origin: Round 4, 2016 Draft (#114 overall)

YEAR	TEAM	LVL	AGE	W	L	SV	G	GS	IP	H	HR	BB/9	K/9	K	GB%	BABIP
2016	TRI	A-	23	0	2	1	14	10	40	27	0	0.4	11.9	53	58%	.293
2017	LEL	A+	24	6	4	0	14	14	78^2	56	9	2.2	10.9	95	53%	.251
2017	SAN	AA	24	5	3	1	10	9	60^1	46	3	2.1	7.9	53	50%	.259
2018	SDN	MLB	25	8	9	0	26	26	130	125	23	3.0	10.0	145	47%	.307
2019	SDN	MLB	26	8	8	0	26	26	130	115	16	2.8	9.5	138	46%	.290

Breakout: 28%   Improve: 52%   Collapse: 14%   Attrition: 14%   MLB: 92%
Comparables: Shaun Marcum, Felipe Paulino, James Shields

Lucchesi is an odd duck on the mound. He's very flexible, and his delivery has a Gumby-like flavor to it, as he twists his shoulders, rocks back and slings himself toward the plate. The weird doesn't stop there. His primary offspeed pitch is what he calls a "churve," a unique cross between a change and curveball that nobody else throws. He grips and throws it like a changeup, but the ball's flight pattern more closely resembles a slider, with modest two-plane action that moves slightly away from lefties and into righties.

It's fair to call the churve a bit of a trick, as long as we also acknowledge that it's a pretty good one. Last year, Lucchesi enticed a whiff 20 percent of the time he threw his trademark, and he rode that and a low-90s fastball to a very effective rookie campaign. Oftentimes, pitchers with one trick face much tougher sledding the second time around the league (think Tony Cingrani and his ubiquitous four-seamer). The onus is on Lucchesi to prove his churve can still miss bats when hitters have first-hand knowledge of how it behaves.

YEAR	TEAM	LVL	AGE	WHIP	ERA	DRA	WARP	MPH	FB%	WHF	CSP
2016	TRI	A-	23	0.73	1.35	1.59	1.7				
2017	LEL	A+	24	0.95	2.52	2.21	2.8				
2017	SAN	AA	24	0.99	1.79	4.09	0.8				
2018	SDN	MLB	25	1.29	4.08	3.79	2.3	92.3	64.1	11.5	49.9
2019	SDN	MLB	26	1.19	3.61	3.87	1.8	91.9	65.3	11.7	50.8

San Diego Padres 2019

Joey Lucchesi, continued

Pitch Shape vs LHH

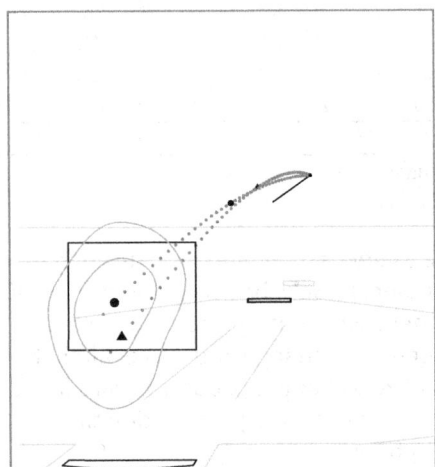

Pitch Shape vs RHH

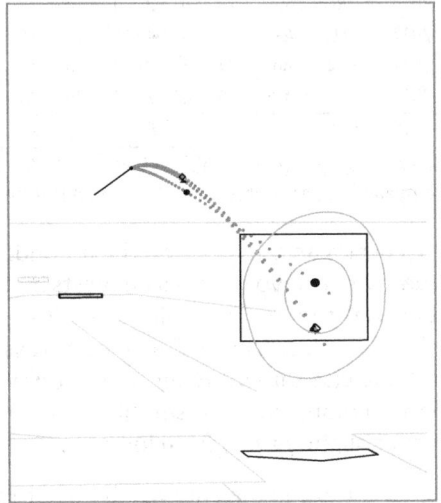

Type	Frequency	Velocity	H Movement	V Movement
● Fastball	64.1%	91.1 [95]	10.6 [82]	-18.9 [90]
☐ Sinker				
+ Cutter				
▲ Changeup	32.1%	79.8 [78]	-0.9 [165]	-38.7 [66]
✕ Splitter				
▽ Slider				
◇ Curveball	3.8%	79.3 [103]	-1.4 [73]	-39.7 [119]
⊕ Slow Curveball				
✱ Knuckleball				
▼ Screwball				

Phil Maton   RHP

Born: 03/25/93   Age: 26   Bats: R   Throws: R
Height: 6'3"   Weight: 220   Origin: Round 20, 2015 Draft (#597 overall)

YEAR	TEAM	LVL	AGE	W	L	SV	G	GS	IP	H	HR	BB/9	K/9	K	GB%	BABIP
2016	FTW	A	23	1	1	1	8	0	12^2	14	0	0.7	13.5	19	33%	.424
2016	LEL	A+	23	3	2	9	25	0	33	17	2	2.2	12.8	47	39%	.217
2016	ELP	AAA	23	1	0	1	5	0	6	1	1	3.0	18.0	12	14%	.000
2017	ELP	AAA	24	1	1	13	23	0	25^1	22	1	2.8	11.0	31	38%	.328
2017	SDN	MLB	24	3	2	1	46	0	43	41	10	2.9	9.6	46	47%	.284
2018	ELP	AAA	25	0	0	2	6	0	6^1	5	0	1.4	14.2	10	40%	.333
2018	SDN	MLB	25	0	2	0	45	0	47^1	50	3	4.4	10.5	55	37%	.359
2019	SDN	MLB	26	2	2	0	36	0	38	36	6	4.0	10.1	43	39%	.300

Breakout: 22%   Improve: 42%   Collapse: 18%   Attrition: 26%   MLB: 73%
Comparables: Nick Goody, Chasen Shreve, Jordan Walden

Analysts and scouts have long sought to identify why some pitchers with mediocre velocity survive in the big leagues while most of their peers peak in A-ball. The answer is typically some alchemical combination of elite command, deception, and guts. Recently, another explanation has come into vogue: spin. To simplify, the more a breaking ball or four-seamer spins (rotates) on its way to the plate, the harder these pitches are to hit. Maton's spin rates are off the charts for a guy who sits in the low-90s, and he's able to entice far more whiffs than most hurlers in his velo band. Tenuous as it sounds, the amount of rotation Maton is able to put on the ball when it leaves his fingers has helped him develop from a 20th-round pick to the 24th man on a big league roster. Youngsters understandably want to ask the stars of the game for tips; perhaps they should be asking Maton how he holds and throws his fastball instead.

YEAR	TEAM	LVL	AGE	WHIP	ERA	DRA	WARP	MPH	FB%	WHF	CSP
2016	FTW	A	23	1.18	1.42	1.53	0.5				
2016	LEL	A+	23	0.76	1.91	2.47	1.0				
2016	ELP	AAA	23	0.50	1.50	1.83	0.2				
2017	ELP	AAA	24	1.18	2.84	3.87	0.4				
2017	SDN	MLB	24	1.28	4.19	3.99	0.6	94.4	76	14.1	50.9
2018	ELP	AAA	25	0.95	2.84	2.62	0.2				
2018	SDN	MLB	25	1.54	4.37	4.42	0.3	92.9	61.2	15.3	43.5
2019	SDN	MLB	26	1.39	4.29	4.50	0.1	93.2	68.5	15.1	47.6

San Diego Padres 2019

Phil Maton, continued

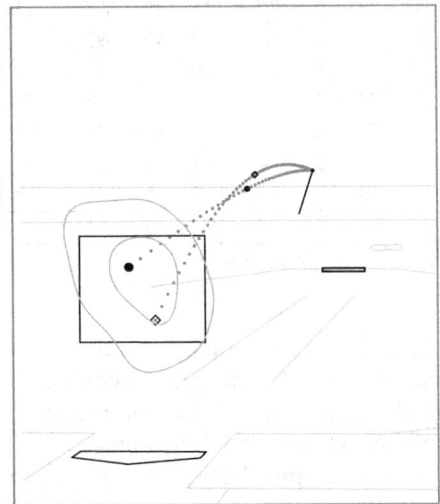
Pitch Shape vs LHH

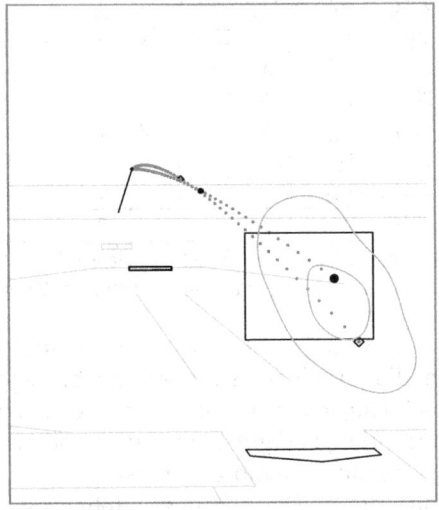
Pitch Shape vs RHH

Type	Frequency	Velocity	H Movement	V Movement
● Fastball	61.2%	91.8 [98]	1.3 [137]	-17.4 [95]
□ Sinker				
+ Cutter				
▲ Changeup				
× Splitter				
▽ Slider				
◇ Curveball	38.8%	79.3 [103]	15.8 [134]	-43.6 [110]
⊕ Slow Curveball				
✱ Knuckleball				
▼ Screwball				

Bryan Mitchell RHP

Born: 04/19/91 Age: 28 Bats: L Throws: R
Height: 6'3" Weight: 210 Origin: Round 16, 2009 Draft (#495 overall)

YEAR	TEAM	LVL	AGE	W	L	SV	G	GS	IP	H	HR	BB/9	K/9	K	GB%	BABIP
2016	SWB	AAA	25	0	0	0	2	2	9	8	0	2.0	14.0	14	50%	.400
2016	NYA	MLB	25	1	2	0	5	5	25	26	1	4.3	4.0	11	49%	.301
2017	SWB	AAA	26	3	3	0	14	13	63^2	59	1	1.8	9.3	66	54%	.326
2017	NYA	MLB	26	1	1	1	20	1	32^2	42	2	3.6	4.7	17	55%	.333
2018	LEL	A+	27	1	3	0	6	6	28^1	23	6	3.8	8.9	28	44%	.239
2018	SDN	MLB	27	2	4	0	16	11	73	85	12	5.3	4.7	38	49%	.302
2019	SDN	MLB	28	4	6	0	31	13	84	92	11	4.3	6.5	61	47%	.302

Breakout: 12% Improve: 29% Collapse: 14% Attrition: 33% MLB: 60%
Comparables: Darrell Rasner, Clay Hensley, Chris Bassitt

Have you ever watched a swimming race until the very end, and noticed how long it takes for the last guy or gal to tap the wall? On some level, you know that that person is an amazing swimmer, one of the best in the world at a pretty difficult task. But, also, they finished last, by a good distance, crawling across the screen much slower than Mr. Phelps or Ms. Ledecky, conspicuous only in how badly they have failed relative to their peers.

Mitchell is the pitching equivalent of that swimmer. He posted a DRA north of 7, a FIP above 6. His earned run average looks merely bad, but if you adjust for a righty pitching in Petco, a 5.42 ERA is pretty ghastly as well. He was one of only two pitchers (minimum 50 innings) to walk more hitters than he struck out. That Mitchell was still starting games in September suggests a science experiment, or at least a concession to draft position. You know he isn't *bad* at this; his presence on a big league roster at all says as much. Sometimes though, being "one of the best in the world" isn't quite good enough.

YEAR	TEAM	LVL	AGE	WHIP	ERA	DRA	WARP	MPH	FB%	WHF	CSP
2016	SWB	AAA	25	1.11	1.00	3.37	0.2				
2016	NYA	MLB	25	1.52	3.24	6.85	-0.4	96.9	50.5	6.7	48.2
2017	SWB	AAA	26	1.13	3.25	3.98	1.2				
2017	NYA	MLB	26	1.68	5.79	5.87	-0.2	97.2	48	7.6	50.3
2018	LEL	A+	27	1.24	4.13	4.56	0.3				
2018	SDN	MLB	27	1.75	5.42	7.10	-1.6	95.5	59.2	6.6	49.1
2019	SDN	MLB	28	1.58	4.99	5.22	-0.2	95.5	55.8	6.9	49.6

San Diego Padres 2019

Bryan Mitchell, continued

Pitch Shape vs LHH
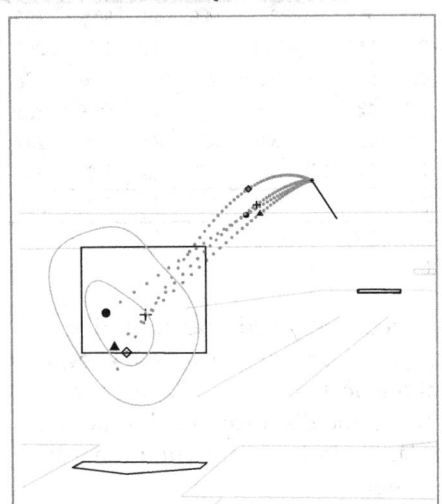

Pitch Shape vs RHH
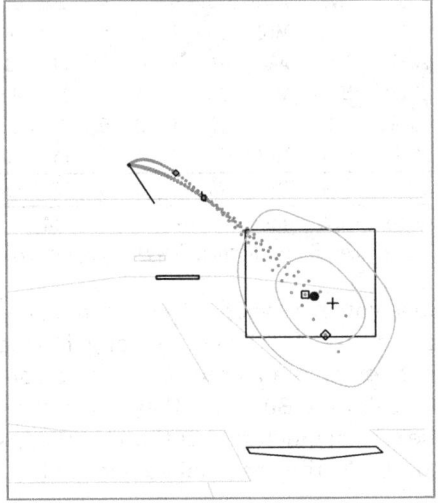

Type	Frequency	Velocity	H Movement	V Movement
● Fastball	52.8%	94.8 [107]	-10.1 [84]	-14.6 [104]
☐ Sinker	6.3%	94.6 [111]	-12.3 [103]	-15.4 [116]
+ Cutter	16.4%	90.9 [112]	-0.7 [85]	-21.6 [109]
▲ Changeup	6.3%	88.5 [113]	-13 [91]	-22.1 [115]
✕ Splitter				
▽ Slider				
◇ Curveball	18.2%	80.4 [107]	10.4 [111]	-47.3 [102]
⊕ Slow Curveball				
✳ Knuckleball				
▼ Screwball				

Jacob Nix RHP

Born: 01/09/96 Age: 23 Bats: R Throws: R
Height: 6'4" Weight: 220 Origin: Round 3, 2015 Draft (#86 overall)

YEAR	TEAM	LVL	AGE	W	L	SV	G	GS	IP	H	HR	BB/9	K/9	K	GB%	BABIP
2016	FTW	A	20	3	7	0	25	25	105^1	115	5	1.7	7.7	90	48%	.340
2017	LEL	A+	21	4	3	0	11	10	66^2	78	5	1.4	6.9	51	48%	.344
2017	SAN	AA	21	1	2	0	6	6	27^2	32	0	2.9	7.2	22	45%	.340
2018	SAN	AA	22	2	3	0	9	9	52^2	39	3	1.5	7.0	41	46%	.250
2018	ELP	AAA	22	1	0	0	1	1	6	5	0	0.0	4.5	3	44%	.278
2018	SDN	MLB	22	2	5	0	9	9	42^1	52	8	2.8	4.5	21	42%	.306
2019	SDN	MLB	23	5	6	0	18	18	90	97	14	2.8	6.9	69	42%	.296

Breakout: 7%   Improve: 17%   Collapse: 13%   Attrition: 25%   MLB: 33%
Comparables: Zach Eflin, Blake Beavan, Will Smith

On August 28, Nix threw one of the weirdest games in recent memory. Through 8.1 shutout innings, Nix had neither struck out a batter nor allowed a walk, an almost impossible accomplishment in modern baseball. Alas, a ninth-inning homer prompted Andy Green to lift Nix before he could get his shutout. It's not like Nix was fatigued—he'd only thrown 79(!) pitches when he came out of the game—but perhaps Green sensed that the guy who can't miss a bat isn't the best option for a one-run game in the ninth. To that last point: Nix struck out less than a batter every two innings, and posted the lowest K/9 of any National Leaguer who threw at least 40 frames. That won't work in the long run. He throws four pitches, all of which have their merits, but if he can't find a way to entice a few more whiffs, he'll be short for this world.

YEAR	TEAM	LVL	AGE	WHIP	ERA	DRA	WARP	MPH	FB%	WHF	CSP
2016	FTW	A	20	1.28	3.93	4.23	1.0				
2017	LEL	A+	21	1.32	4.32	5.01	0.2				
2017	SAN	AA	21	1.48	5.53	6.85	-0.6				
2018	SAN	AA	22	0.91	2.05	3.86	0.9				
2018	ELP	AAA	22	0.83	0.00	4.12	0.1				
2018	SDN	MLB	22	1.54	7.02	6.94	-0.8	94.6	62.5	6.7	49.7
2019	SDN	MLB	23	1.39	4.70	5.03	0.0	94.5	64.7	7	51.5

San Diego Padres 2019

Jacob Nix, continued

Pitch Shape vs LHH
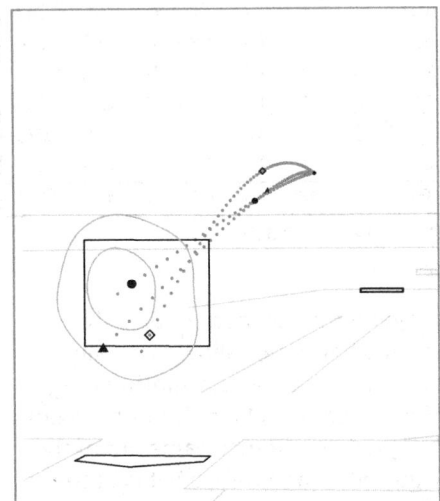

Pitch Shape vs RHH
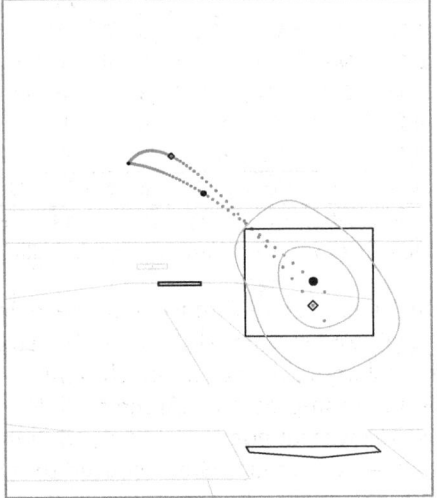

Type	Frequency	Velocity	H Movement	V Movement
● Fastball	62.5%	93.6 [104]	-8.4 [92]	-14.7 [103]
☐ Sinker				
+ Cutter				
▲ Changeup	14.2%	81.2 [83]	-14.8 [81]	-35.5 [76]
✕ Splitter				
▽ Slider	3.7%	81.7 [88]	4.6 [99]	-37.9 [85]
◇ Curveball	19.7%	77.4 [96]	8.1 [101]	-54.4 [86]
⊕ Slow Curveball				
✳ Knuckleball				
▼ Screwball				

Luis Perdomo   RHP

Born: 05/09/93   Age: 26   Bats: R   Throws: R
Height: 6'2"   Weight: 185   Origin: International Free Agent, 2003

YEAR	TEAM	LVL	AGE	W	L	SV	G	GS	IP	H	HR	BB/9	K/9	K	GB%	BABIP
2016	SDN	MLB	23	9	10	0	35	20	146²	187	23	2.8	6.4	105	60%	.342
2017	SDN	MLB	24	8	11	0	29	29	163²	182	17	3.6	6.5	118	62%	.325
2018	ELP	AAA	25	6	3	0	13	13	75	72	12	2.5	7.3	61	57%	.284
2018	SDN	MLB	25	1	6	0	12	10	44²	62	4	4.4	7.9	39	44%	.389
2019	SDN	MLB	26	5	5	0	31	13	87	93	10	3.6	7.4	72	53%	.310

Breakout: 33%   Improve: 62%   Collapse: 17%   Attrition: 14%   MLB: 88%
Comparables: Jacob Turner, Billy Traber, Luke Hochevar

For anyone wondering why baseball doesn't have more pitchers like Mike Leake or Jose Fernandez, guys who can skip from college or A-ball to the majors, just look at Perdomo. Tall, athletic, and armed with a nasty mid-90s two-seamer and a wipeout slider, Perdomo has most of the ingredients a major league pitcher needs. If any Rule 5 pick could jump from High-A to the majors, he seemed like a decent bet.

Unfortunately for Perdomo, it takes more than an ideal frame and good stuff to get big leaguers out. Back in A-ball, Perdomo was still learning how to deploy his arsenal: The art of sequencing, the finer points of the changeup, when to nibble. How to *pitch*, basically. Those are hard lessons to learn on the big stage, and the Padres finally ran out of patience. It's possible that last year's demotion gave him the reset he badly needs; it's perhaps more likely that the lost developmental time has already sunk his hopes of a lasting big league career.

YEAR	TEAM	LVL	AGE	WHIP	ERA	DRA	WARP	MPH	FB%	WHF	CSP
2016	SDN	MLB	23	1.59	5.71	5.29	0.0	96.4	68.3	9	48.6
2017	SDN	MLB	24	1.51	4.67	4.96	1.1	95.9	62.8	9.6	47.1
2018	ELP	AAA	25	1.24	3.72	3.91	1.4				
2018	SDN	MLB	25	1.88	7.05	6.52	-0.6	95.0	63	8	47.1
2019	SDN	MLB	26	1.49	4.23	4.51	0.5	95.5	65.8	9.3	48.3

San Diego Padres 2019

Luis Perdomo, continued

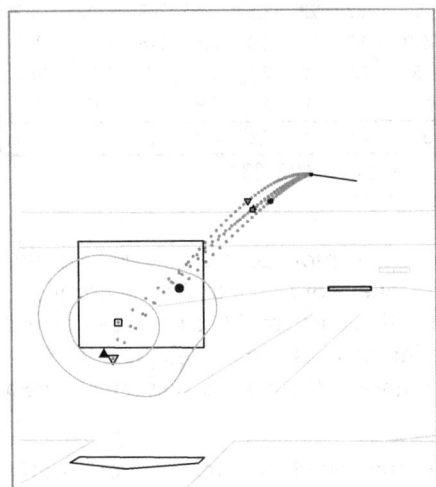
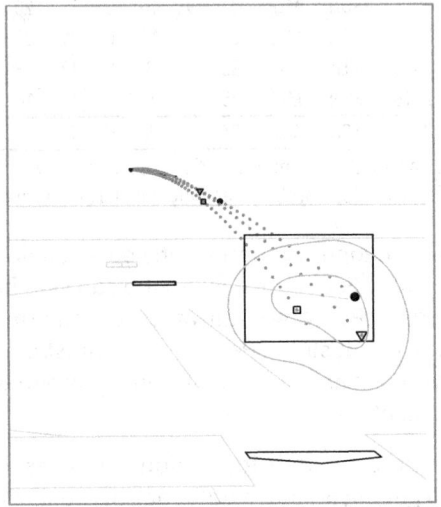

Type	Frequency	Velocity	H Movement	V Movement
● Fastball	10.3%	94.1 [105]	-8.6 [91]	-16 [99]
□ Sinker	52.7%	93.9 [107]	-13.4 [93]	-21 [98]
+ Cutter				
▲ Changeup	9.9%	87.7 [110]	-11.8 [97]	-27.6 [99]
× Splitter	0.5%	87.6 [111]	-13.2 [81]	-29.1 [102]
▽ Slider	22.9%	86.3 [108]	1.7 [86]	-32.9 [100]
◇ Curveball	3.6%	84.9 [124]	2.6 [78]	-36.1 [127]
⊕ Slow Curveball				
✴ Knuckleball				
▼ Screwball				

Garrett Richards   RHP

Born: 05/27/88   Age: 31   Bats: R   Throws: R
Height: 6'3"   Weight: 210   Origin: Round 1, 2009 Draft (#42 overall)

YEAR	TEAM	LVL	AGE	W	L	SV	G	GS	IP	H	HR	BB/9	K/9	K	GB%	BABIP
2016	ANA	MLB	28	1	3	0	6	6	34^2	31	2	3.9	8.8	34	47%	.302
2017	ANA	MLB	29	0	2	0	6	6	27^2	18	1	2.3	8.8	27	55%	.233
2018	ANA	MLB	30	5	4	0	16	16	76^1	64	11	4.0	10.3	87	50%	.277
2019	SDN	MLB	31	4	3	0	11	11	63^1	52	6	3.8	9.8	69	48%	.299

Breakout: 10%   Improve: 31%   Collapse: 28%   Attrition: 6%   MLB: 88%
Comparables: C.J. Wilson, Tim Hudson, Bob Veale

The general knowledge trivia website LearnedLeague has a term for players who forfeit so many times in a season that they are ineligible to play the next season: it's called a pavano, named after the pitcher who threw 26 games in his four years with the Yankees. Richards effectively pavanoed the completion of his Angels tenure, managing 28 starts in a four-year span. That total includes 2019, which he will miss to Tommy John surgery—his first (though his second UCL injury; the team tried to avoid surgery the first time around). Unlike Pavano, who was ineffective even when active, Richards' absence made the Angels' heart grow fonder. The Padres, reading the winds on their voyage to contention, decided to make Richards part of their 2020 playoff run, signing him to a two-year, $15.5 million deal.

YEAR	TEAM	LVL	AGE	WHIP	ERA	DRA	WARP	MPH	FB%	WHF	CSP
2016	ANA	MLB	28	1.33	2.34	4.42	0.4	98.5	62.4	11.3	43.5
2017	ANA	MLB	29	0.90	2.28	3.12	0.8	97.2	58.2	13.2	43.8
2018	ANA	MLB	30	1.28	3.66	3.73	1.4	97.5	50.4	12.3	47.5
2019	SDN	MLB	31	1.25	3.46	3.85	1.1	96.7	53.6	12.2	45

San Diego Padres 2019

Garrett Richards, continued

Pitch Shape vs LHH

Pitch Shape vs RHH

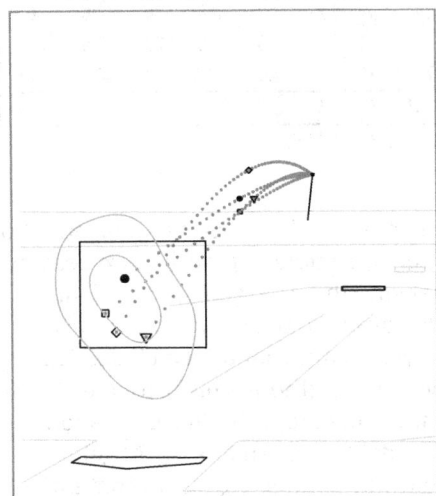
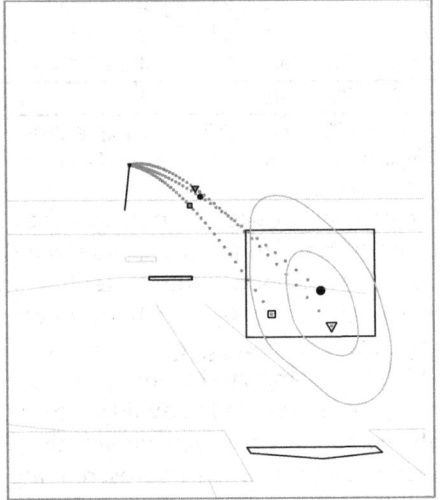

Type	Frequency	Velocity	H Movement	V Movement
● Fastball	32.4%	96.3 [112]	1.7 [138]	-17.3 [95]
□ Sinker	18.0%	96.4 [120]	-7.2 [144]	-17.7 [109]
+ Cutter				
▲ Changeup	0.1%	91.8 [126]	-18.3 [63]	-30.7 [90]
× Splitter				
▽ Slider	38.9%	89.6 [123]	2.5 [90]	-34.3 [96]
◇ Curveball	10.6%	81.5 [111]	8 [101]	-56.8 [80]
⊕ Slow Curveball				
✱ Knuckleball				
▼ Screwball				

68 - Padres Player Analysis

Craig Stammen   RHP

Born: 03/09/84   Age: 35   Bats: R   Throws: R
Height: 6'4"   Weight: 230   Origin: Round 12, 2005 Draft (#354 overall)

YEAR	TEAM	LVL	AGE	W	L	SV	G	GS	IP	H	HR	BB/9	K/9	K	GB%	BABIP
2016	AKR	AA	32	0	1	0	10	0	11^1	9	1	2.4	7.1	9	69%	.235
2016	COH	AAA	32	0	3	0	10	0	13	16	2	1.4	7.6	11	57%	.333
2017	SDN	MLB	33	2	3	0	60	0	80^1	68	12	3.1	8.3	74	52%	.263
2018	SDN	MLB	34	8	3	0	73	0	79	65	3	1.9	10.0	88	51%	.301
2019	SDN	MLB	35	3	3	2	60	0	63	60	8	3.5	8.9	63	50%	.297

Breakout: 23%   Improve: 40%   Collapse: 25%   Attrition: 13%   MLB: 83%
Comparables: Scott Downs, Brian Duensing, Ryan Madson

Ever watched someone play and had a sudden impulse to see what their Twitter feed looked like? Such was the case for this humble author one summer night in 2012. Turns out, it was a pretty standard athlete profile—quotes from Scripture, some golf, shoutouts to the fans and the troops—not substantively different from his more famous teammates, just at two percent of the volume. Six years later, his posting habits haven't changed much and he's still quietly running an ERA in the mid-2s. In between he's had Tommy John surgery, got married, watched his wife go viral after notching a hole in one on their honeymoon, signed the first two-year deal of his life and sired a child. Not to get overly meta here, but the whole experience has me reflecting on just how little we really know about these people we share so much of our time with.

YEAR	TEAM	LVL	AGE	WHIP	ERA	DRA	WARP	MPH	FB%	WHF	CSP
2016	AKR	AA	32	1.06	0.79	2.64	0.3				
2016	COH	AAA	32	1.38	5.54	3.73	0.2				
2017	SDN	MLB	33	1.20	3.14	3.76	1.3	92.7	63.3	12.2	44.1
2018	SDN	MLB	34	1.04	2.73	2.86	1.9	93.4	67.6	14.6	47
2019	SDN	MLB	35	1.33	4.06	4.32	0.4	91.9	64.4	13.3	44.9

San Diego Padres 2019

Craig Stammen, continued

Pitch Shape vs LHH
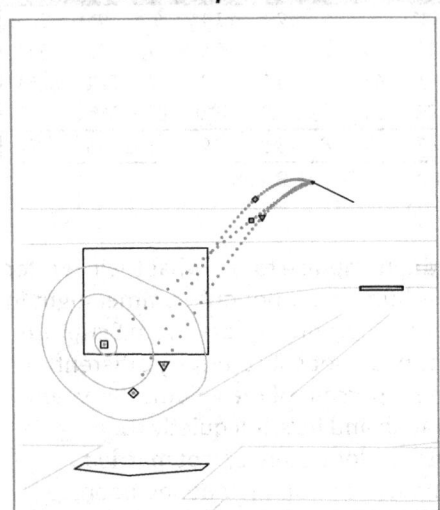

Pitch Shape vs RHH
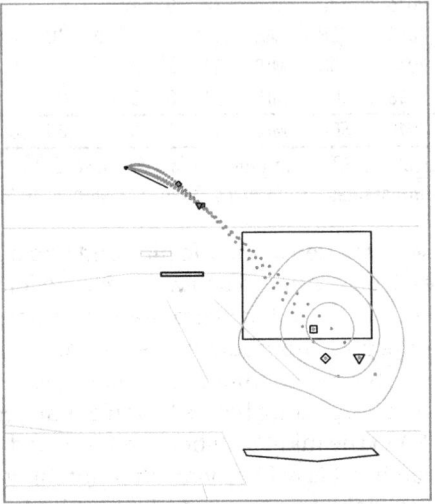

Type	Frequency	Velocity	H Movement	V Movement
● Fastball	2.8%	92.2 [99]	-9.6 [87]	-16.4 [98]
□ Sinker	64.8%	92.3 [99]	-12.5 [101]	-20 [101]
+ Cutter				
▲ Changeup	0.7%	89.4 [116]	-11.5 [99]	-20.8 [119]
× Splitter				
▽ Slider	20.7%	87.5 [113]	2.4 [89]	-27.2 [117]
◇ Curveball	11.0%	81.5 [111]	7.4 [98]	-46.9 [103]
⊕ Slow Curveball				
✳ Knuckleball				
▼ Screwball				

Robert Stock RHP

Born: 11/21/89   Age: 29   Bats: L   Throws: R
Height: 6'1"   Weight: 214   Origin: Round 2, 2009 Draft (#67 overall)

YEAR	TEAM	LVL	AGE	W	L	SV	G	GS	IP	H	HR	BB/9	K/9	K	GB%	BABIP
2017	DAY	A+	27	1	3	2	16	0	25	18	1	2.9	9.0	25	55%	.279
2017	PEN	AA	27	8	2	0	25	0	45^1	39	0	4.2	7.1	36	55%	.307
2018	SAN	AA	28	1	0	1	8	0	9	7	1	3.0	15.0	15	40%	.316
2018	ELP	AAA	28	0	0	8	24	0	28^1	15	2	3.5	8.6	27	59%	.183
2018	SDN	MLB	28	1	1	0	32	0	39^2	37	1	2.9	8.6	38	51%	.321
2019	SDN	MLB	29	3	3	0	54	0	57	55	7	4.4	8.3	53	49%	.296

Breakout: 12%   Improve: 22%   Collapse: 15%   Attrition: 19%   MLB: 39%
Comparables: Cody Eppley, Joe Paterson, Josh Roenicke

A minor league journeyman with indy ball experience on his resume, Stock emerged from obscurity toting a triple-digit fastball; he soon established himself as one of San Diego's most reliable relievers. Stock is one of a growing number of pitchers who have dramatically altered their career trajectory by trying to throw every pitch through a brick wall and letting the chips fall where they may from there. These players, easily identifiable by their violent deliveries and velo-evangelizing tweets, are often too wild to be effective. Stock throws plenty of strikes though, and while his command needs refinement, hitters weren't able to regularly barrel his elite gas. It appears the Padres found a legitimate late-inning arm out of nowhere.

YEAR	TEAM	LVL	AGE	WHIP	ERA	DRA	WARP	MPH	FB%	WHF	CSP
2017	DAY	A+	27	1.04	2.52	3.22	0.5				
2017	PEN	AA	27	1.32	2.98	4.84	0.0				
2018	SAN	AA	28	1.11	2.00	2.38	0.3				
2018	ELP	AAA	28	0.92	1.59	2.95	0.7				
2018	SDN	MLB	28	1.26	2.50	3.51	0.6	99.4	59	10.8	50.4
2019	SDN	MLB	29	1.45	4.54	4.70	0.1	98.7	59	10.8	50.4

Robert Stock, continued

Pitch Shape vs LHH
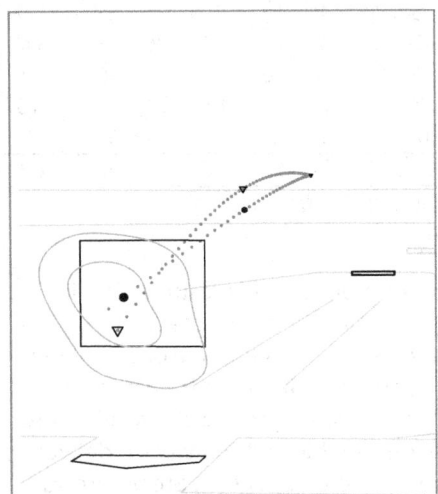

Pitch Shape vs RHH
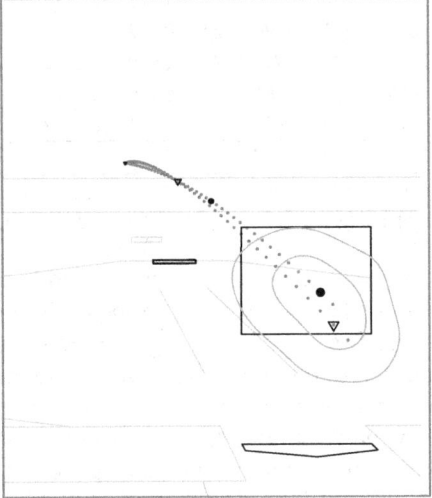

Type	Frequency	Velocity	H Movement	V Movement
● Fastball	58.9%	98.2 [118]	-9.8 [86]	-15.5 [101]
☐ Sinker				
+ Cutter				
▲ Changeup	3.8%	83.2 [92]	-11.8 [97]	-28.6 [96]
✕ Splitter				
▽ Slider	37.3%	83.3 [95]	11.8 [130]	-35.8 [92]
◇ Curveball				
⊕ Slow Curveball				
✳ Knuckleball				
▼ Screwball				

Matt Strahm LHP

Born: 11/12/91 Age: 27 Bats: R Throws: L
Height: 6'3" Weight: 185 Origin: Round 21, 2012 Draft (#643 overall)

YEAR	TEAM	LVL	AGE	W	L	SV	G	GS	IP	H	HR	BB/9	K/9	K	GB%	BABIP
2016	NWA	AA	24	3	8	0	22	18	102¹	102	14	2.0	9.4	107	40%	.320
2016	KCA	MLB	24	2	2	0	21	0	22	13	0	4.5	12.3	30	50%	.283
2017	KCA	MLB	25	2	5	0	24	3	34²	30	6	5.7	9.6	37	42%	.279
2018	SAN	AA	26	1	0	0	9	2	14¹	14	1	2.5	13.8	22	42%	.406
2018	SDN	MLB	26	3	4	0	41	5	61¹	39	6	3.1	10.1	69	37%	.226
2019	SDN	MLB	27	5	6	0	43	13	92	86	13	3.7	9.6	99	40%	.296

Breakout: 22% Improve: 45% Collapse: 19% Attrition: 21% MLB: 81%
Comparables: Scott Elbert, Jose Capellan, Zack Godley

If it seems like you've read about a dozen or so quality relievers by this point, you're not mistaken. San Diego upheld its reputation as a reliever factory by producing one of the best bullpens in the league last year and the club didn't miss a beat after dealing Adam Cimber and closer Brad Hand to Cleveland last summer. Part of that is because of Strahm, who ran with his new role after a promotion to late-inning duty in August. Over the final two months, Strahm posted a 1.25 ERA with 30 punchouts and only six walks in 21 innings. Both Kansas City and San Diego have experimented with stretching him out but after last year's success in relief, it appears he's found his home.

YEAR	TEAM	LVL	AGE	WHIP	ERA	DRA	WARP	MPH	FB%	WHF	CSP
2016	NWA	AA	24	1.22	3.43	4.73	0.4				
2016	KCA	MLB	24	1.09	1.23	4.13	0.2	96.8	77.9	14.1	43.2
2017	KCA	MLB	25	1.50	5.45	5.80	-0.2	95.7	67.3	11.2	49.1
2018	SAN	AA	26	1.26	2.51	3.54	0.3				
2018	SDN	MLB	26	0.98	2.05	3.96	0.7	95.5	58	13.3	52.9
2019	SDN	MLB	27	1.34	4.19	4.46	0.5	95.2	64.4	13	49.8

San Diego Padres 2019

Matt Strahm, continued

Pitch Shape vs LHH
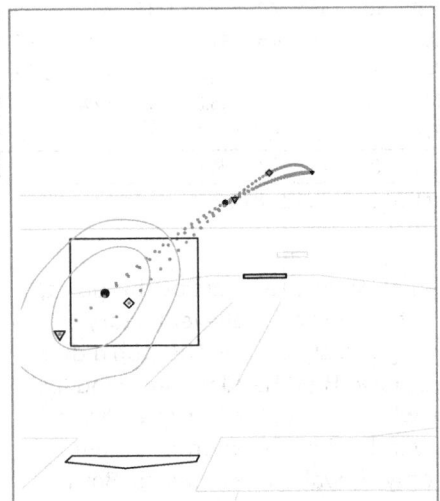

Pitch Shape vs RHH
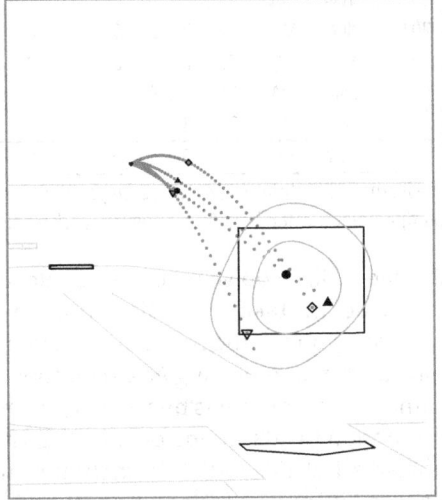

Type	Frequency	Velocity	H Movement	V Movement
● Fastball	58.0%	94 [105]	11.9 [76]	-15.4 [101]
☐ Sinker				
+ Cutter				
▲ Changeup	14.3%	86.5 [105]	16 [75]	-29.2 [94]
✕ Splitter				
▽ Slider	15.3%	87.6 [114]	-4.5 [99]	-28.4 [114]
◇ Curveball	12.3%	78.4 [100]	-11.2 [114]	-44.6 [108]
⊕ Slow Curveball				
✱ Knuckleball				
▼ Screwball				

Adam Warren   RHP

Born: 08/25/87   Age: 31   Bats: R   Throws: R
Height: 6'1"   Weight: 224   Origin: Round 4, 2009 Draft (#135 overall)

YEAR	TEAM	LVL	AGE	W	L	SV	G	GS	IP	H	HR	BB/9	K/9	K	GB%	BABIP
2016	IOW	AAA	28	0	0	0	2	2	8^2	6	1	4.2	6.2	6	38%	.217
2016	CHN	MLB	28	3	2	0	29	1	35	31	7	4.9	6.9	27	44%	.242
2016	NYA	MLB	28	4	2	0	29	0	30^1	28	4	3.0	7.4	25	45%	.282
2017	NYA	MLB	29	3	2	1	46	0	57^1	35	4	2.4	8.5	54	44%	.208
2018	NYA	MLB	30	0	1	0	24	0	30	26	3	3.6	11.1	37	37%	.307
2018	SEA	MLB	30	3	1	0	23	0	21^2	22	3	3.3	6.2	15	39%	.279
2019	SDN	MLB	31	3	3	0	60	0	63	58	8	4.0	8.6	61	42%	.285

Breakout: 20%   Improve: 42%   Collapse: 28%   Attrition: 10%   MLB: 90%
Comparables: Ramon Ramirez, Jim Johnson, Justin Duchscherer

History has no record of Warren prior to his appearance in the Yankees' bullpen in 2012. There are claims that he played college baseball with Kyle Seager and Dustin Ackley at North Carolina, but witnesses couldn't corroborate. Seager was unavailable for comment, while Ackley simply responded with an eternally blank stare and silence. Still, consider the facts: Since his debut Warren has been largely effective as long as he wears the black pinstripes. The second he dons another uniform, as he did in 2016 for the Cubs, and last year for the Mariners, everything falls apart. Does this mean the Yankees, with all their immense wealth and access to technology, have begun manufacturing smooth-shaven androids, nefarious sleeper agents designed to malfunction and fail the second they leave the Bronx? Is this baseball's next great conspiracy? Unfortunately, for the purposes of this player comment, Brian Cashman did not return our calls, and also barred us from his favorite restaurant, the TGI Fridays in Times Square.

YEAR	TEAM	LVL	AGE	WHIP	ERA	DRA	WARP	MPH	FB%	WHF	CSP
2016	IOW	AAA	28	1.15	4.15	4.63	0.1				
2016	CHN	MLB	28	1.43	5.91	4.16	0.3	95.3	45	11.9	43.1
2016	NYA	MLB	28	1.25	3.26	6.46	-0.5	94.9	42	10.2	44.6
2017	NYA	MLB	29	0.87	2.35	3.01	1.4	94.1	38.9	10.7	42.5
2018	NYA	MLB	30	1.27	2.70	3.27	0.6	93.0	39	12	38.6
2018	SEA	MLB	30	1.38	3.74	5.44	-0.1	93.7	41.7	10.4	44.2
2019	SDN	MLB	31	1.35	4.51	4.68	0.1	93.2	40.5	11	41.9

San Diego Padres 2019

Adam Warren, continued

Pitch Shape vs LHH
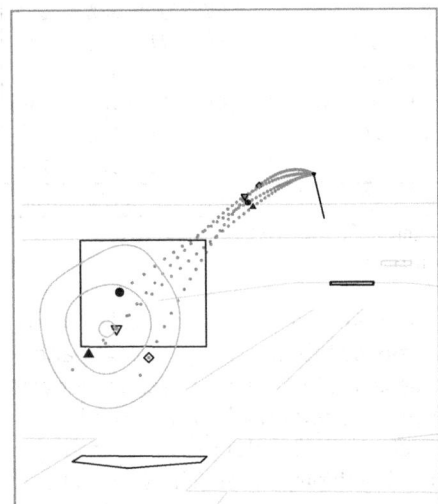

Pitch Shape vs RHH
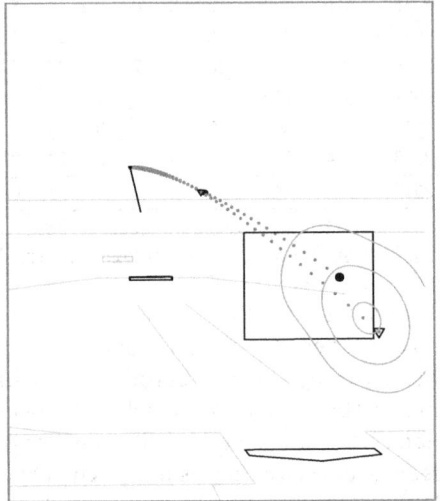

Type	Frequency	Velocity	H Movement	V Movement
● Fastball	40.0%	92.3 [99]	-2.8 [118]	-14.1 [105]
□ Sinker	0.1%	93.6 [106]	-14 [89]	-11.6 [129]
+ Cutter				
▲ Changeup	8.3%	85.1 [99]	-13.5 [88]	-28.2 [97]
✕ Splitter				
▽ Slider	45.4%	85.6 [105]	6.7 [108]	-30 [109]
◇ Curveball	6.2%	80.5 [107]	6.8 [96]	-47.3 [102]
⊕ Slow Curveball				
✱ Knuckleball				
▼ Screwball				

Trey Wingenter   RHP
Born: 04/15/94   Age: 25   Bats: R   Throws: R
Height: 6'7"   Weight: 200   Origin: Round 17, 2015 Draft (#507 overall)

YEAR	TEAM	LVL	AGE	W	L	SV	G	GS	IP	H	HR	BB/9	K/9	K	GB%	BABIP
2016	FTW	A	22	1	0	4	8	0	11	6	0	1.6	11.5	14	46%	.250
2016	LEL	A+	22	2	1	4	30	0	44^1	36	0	3.5	9.3	46	59%	.321
2017	SAN	AA	23	2	1	20	49	0	47^2	33	6	3.6	12.1	64	52%	.262
2018	ELP	AAA	24	3	3	4	40	0	44^1	29	4	4.9	10.8	53	48%	.250
2018	SDN	MLB	24	0	0	0	22	0	19	13	3	5.2	12.8	27	40%	.256
2019	SDN	MLB	25	3	3	0	60	0	63	53	7	4.8	10.3	73	46%	.292

Breakout: 17%   Improve: 21%   Collapse: 27%   Attrition: 34%   MLB: 52%
Comparables: Keith Butler, Akeel Morris, Joseph Krehbiel

In every rebuilding season, there comes a point when prospect saturation kicks in, when even plugged in fans no longer know anything about the new yannigan trotting in from the bullpen. Wingenter debuted on August 7th, the tenth Padre to do so in 2018, and it would have been easy to gloss over this big-bodied, long-haired, multisyllabic reliever. Wingenter, though, is actually pretty interesting. He sits in the high-90s, regularly touching triple digits, and he pairs the pitch with a sweeping slider. He needs to throw more strikes, but after posting elite whiff rates with both pitches, it looks like he has the raw stuff for late-inning duty.

YEAR	TEAM	LVL	AGE	WHIP	ERA	DRA	WARP	MPH	FB%	WHF	CSP
2016	FTW	A	22	0.73	0.82	2.85	0.2				
2016	LEL	A+	22	1.20	2.03	3.81	0.6				
2017	SAN	AA	23	1.09	2.45	2.44	1.3				
2018	ELP	AAA	24	1.20	3.45	3.56	0.8				
2018	SDN	MLB	24	1.26	3.79	2.84	0.5	99.1	68.6	18.3	49.5
2019	SDN	MLB	25	1.36	4.00	4.27	0.4	98.8	70.3	18.8	50.6

Trey Wingenter, continued

Pitch Shape vs LHH | **Pitch Shape vs RHH**

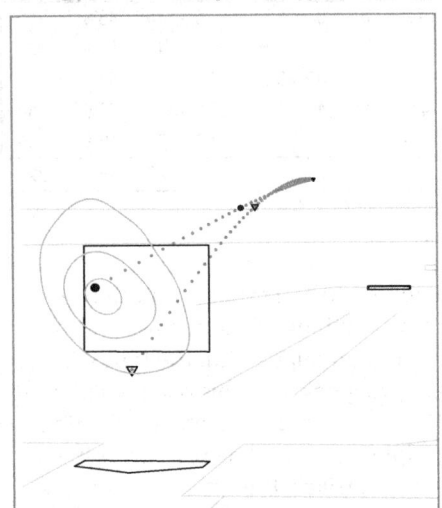 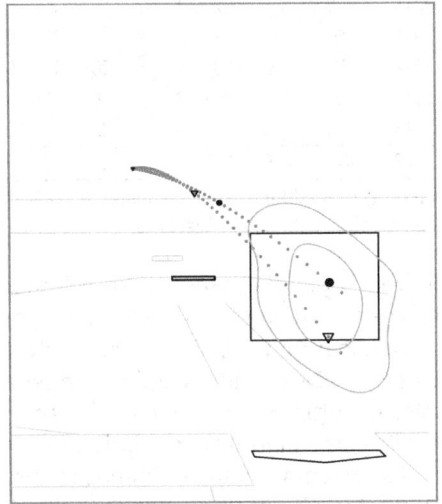

Type	Frequency	Velocity	H Movement	V Movement
● Fastball	68.6%	98.2 [118]	-9.4 [87]	-12.5 [110]
☐ Sinker				
+ Cutter				
▲ Changeup	0.3%	90.7 [121]	-10.4 [105]	-16.9 [131]
✕ Splitter				
▽ Slider	31.1%	86.8 [111]	2.3 [89]	-34.7 [95]
◇ Curveball				
⊕ Slow Curveball				
✳ Knuckleball				
▼ Screwball				

Kirby Yates RHP
Born: 03/25/87   Age: 32   Bats: L   Throws: R
Height: 5'10"   Weight: 210   Origin: Round 26, 2005 Draft (#798 overall)

YEAR	TEAM	LVL	AGE	W	L	SV	G	GS	IP	H	HR	BB/9	K/9	K	GB%	BABIP
2016	SWB	AAA	29	0	1	4	14	0	16²	12	0	3.2	10.3	19	46%	.279
2016	NYA	MLB	29	2	1	0	41	0	41¹	41	5	4.1	10.9	50	44%	.340
2017	SLC	AAA	30	0	0	1	6	0	7	8	0	3.9	18.0	14	60%	.533
2017	ANA	MLB	30	0	0	0	1	0	1	2	2	0.0	9.0	1	0%	.000
2017	SDN	MLB	30	4	5	1	61	0	55²	42	10	3.1	14.1	87	30%	.296
2018	SDN	MLB	31	5	3	12	65	0	63	41	6	2.4	12.9	90	43%	.263
2019	SDN	MLB	32	3	3	35	60	0	63	53	7	3.7	11.6	82	41%	.298

Breakout: 15%   Improve: 34%   Collapse: 23%   Attrition: 8%   MLB: 70%
Comparables: Sergio Santos, Paul Assenmacher, Brian Sikorski

Yates wasn't drafted out of college, needed four years of minor league seasoning and didn't assume closing duties until he was 31. And yet he was born for the role. You can see it in his fiery enthusiasm, populist forename, funky delivery and elite strikeout rate. His splitter is a closer's pitch, enticing an absurd whiff rate (27 percent last year) with late, vanishing action that makes it the kind of pro-wrestling move every fireman needs. That he also has a bit of a homer problem—he surrendered five over the last two months—makes him the best kind of closer, or at least the most watchable for neutrals. If he can limit the gopher balls, he should hang on to his new gig for a few years.

YEAR	TEAM	LVL	AGE	WHIP	ERA	DRA	WARP	MPH	FB%	WHF	CSP
2016	SWB	AAA	29	1.08	1.62	2.17	0.5				
2016	NYA	MLB	29	1.45	5.23	4.07	0.4	95.3	59.9	12.4	45.3
2017	SLC	AAA	30	1.57	2.57	0.20	0.4				
2017	ANA	MLB	30	2.00	18.00	9.07	0.0	94.7	50	12.5	53.8
2017	SDN	MLB	30	1.10	3.72	3.10	1.3	95.0	62.9	18.8	48.3
2018	SDN	MLB	31	0.92	2.14	1.92	2.2	95.3	58.3	18.6	43.2
2019	SDN	MLB	32	1.24	3.12	3.53	0.9	94.2	59.6	17.2	45

San Diego Padres 2019

Kirby Yates, continued

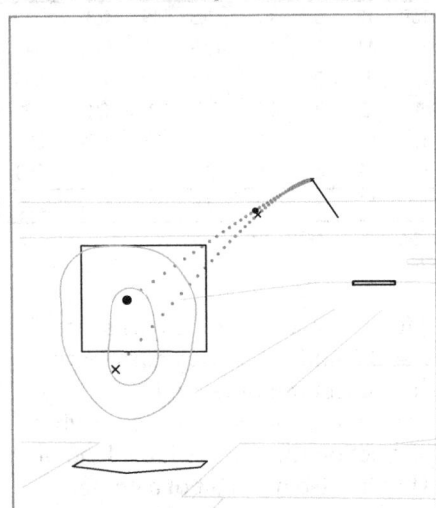
Pitch Shape vs LHH

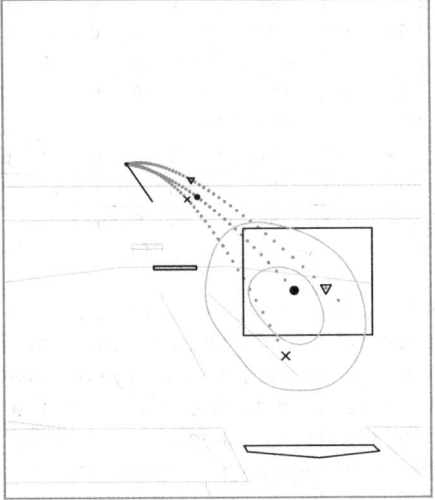
Pitch Shape vs RHH

Type	Frequency	Velocity	H Movement	V Movement
● Fastball	58.3%	94.5 [106]	-11.1 [80]	-14.1 [105]
☐ Sinker				
+ Cutter				
▲ Changeup				
✕ Splitter	37.0%	87.9 [112]	-10.6 [90]	-29.4 [100]
▽ Slider	4.7%	87.3 [113]	0.1 [79]	-27.7 [116]
◇ Curveball				
⊕ Slow Curveball				
✳ Knuckleball				
▼ Screwball				

Xavier Edwards SS

Born: 08/09/99   Age: 19   Bats: B   Throws: R
Height: 5'10"   Weight: 155   Origin: Round 1, 2018 Draft (#38 overall)

YEAR	TEAM	LVL	AGE	PA	R	2B	3B	HR	RBI	BB	K	SB	CS	AVG/OBP/SLG
2018	PDR	RK	18	88	19	4	1	0	11	13	10	12	1	.384/.471/.466
2018	TRI	A-	18	107	21	4	0	0	5	18	15	10	0	.314/.438/.360
2019	SDN	MLB	19	251	28	5	0	5	19	22	60	8	1	.197/.266/.284

Breakout: 7%   Improve: 9%   Collapse: 0%   Attrition: 5%   MLB: 10%
Comparables: Gleyber Torres, Elvis Andrus, Carlos Triunfel

Edwards fell in the draft last June, and the Padres snapped him up with their second first-round selection. He has electric speed and a consistent track record of hitting pretty good amateur competition with a smooth and well-honed line drive swing. At 5-foot-10 and 155 pounds, he's smaller than most draft picks in his orbit, but he's a sure middle infielder with a lot of baseball ability. He doesn't project to hit for much power, but in the Altuve-Betts era, you've got to be at least mildly bullish that an athletic and deceptively strong kid with a great swing and terrific eye finds a way to add that to his game too. Potential oozes everywhere.

YEAR	TEAM	LVL	AGE	PA	DRC+	VORP	BABIP	BRR	FRAA	WARP
2018	PDR	RK	18	88	194	13.5	.438	1.9	SS(15): 3.1	1.2
2018	TRI	A-	18	107	180	9.9	.380	-0.3	SS(19): -1.1, 2B(5): 0.0	0.7
2019	SDN	MLB	19	251	52	-4.6	.241	0.7	SS 0, 2B 0	-0.5

Josh Naylor LF

Born: 06/22/97 Age: 22 Bats: L Throws: L
Height: 5'11" Weight: 250 Origin: Round 1, 2015 Draft (#12 overall)

YEAR	TEAM	LVL	AGE	PA	R	2B	3B	HR	RBI	BB	K	SB	CS	AVG/OBP/SLG
2016	GRB	A	19	370	42	24	2	9	54	22	62	10	3	.269/.317/.430
2016	LEL	A+	19	144	17	5	0	3	21	3	22	1	1	.252/.264/.353
2017	LEL	A+	20	313	41	16	2	8	45	27	48	7	1	.297/.361/.452
2017	SAN	AA	20	175	18	9	0	2	19	16	36	2	1	.250/.320/.346
2018	SAN	AA	21	574	72	22	1	17	74	64	69	5	5	.297/.383/.447
2019	SDN	MLB	22	251	25	9	0	9	30	15	49	1	0	.223/.274/.377

Breakout: 12% Improve: 31% Collapse: 1% Attrition: 19% MLB: 33%
Comparables: Ramon Flores, Dwight Smith, Jake Bauers

Naylor has several promising traits that haven't quite clicked in games yet. The 21-year-old has 70-grade raw power, good barrel control, a decent understanding of the strike zone and a feel for contact. It all plays down, however, because his swing is relatively flat and he's too easily coaxed into weak contact on pitches outside his wheelhouse. There are signs he's snapping out of that to some extent—he hit a career high 17 bombs last year and added a bit of loft to his swing plane—but it's unclear whether San Diego will ever reap the benefits even if he hits: Naylor's physique and lack of speed suggest he's a first basemen all the way. But with Eric Hosmer in tow, he saw plenty of action in left last year, where he (not surprisingly) isn't up to snuff. The ingredients here are good, but you can't make cookies with pizza dough and marinara sauce. Whether that means Naylor needs a change of scenery or something else is for the chefs to determine.

YEAR	TEAM	LVL	AGE	PA	DRC+	VORP	BABIP	BRR	FRAA	WARP
2016	GRB	A	19	370	109	10.5	.304	-1.9	1B(81): -2.3	-0.5
2016	LEL	A+	19	144	55	-2.9	.276	-0.6	1B(32): -3.4	-1.2
2017	LEL	A+	20	313	136	14.6	.333	-0.1	1B(42): -0.6	0.6
2017	SAN	AA	20	175	100	0.6	.308	-0.9	1B(40): 1.9	-0.1
2018	SAN	AA	21	574	139	27.4	.317	-5.1	LF(89): -20.4, 1B(29): 0.6	-0.4
2019	SDN	MLB	22	251	75	-1.6	.244	-0.5	LF -5, 1B 0	-0.7

Hudson Potts 3B

Born: 10/28/98 Age: 20 Bats: R Throws: R
Height: 6'3" Weight: 205 Origin: Round 1, 2016 Draft (#24 overall)

YEAR	TEAM	LVL	AGE	PA	R	2B	3B	HR	RBI	BB	K	SB	CS	AVG/OBP/SLG
2016	PDR	RK	17	195	35	12	2	1	21	9	34	8	4	.295/.333/.399
2016	TRI	A-	17	72	7	0	1	0	6	9	13	2	1	.233/.352/.267
2017	FTW	A	18	522	67	23	4	20	69	23	140	0	1	.253/.293/.438
2018	LEL	A+	19	453	66	35	1	17	58	37	112	3	1	.281/.350/.498
2018	SAN	AA	19	89	5	0	0	2	5	10	33	1	0	.154/.258/.231
2019	SDN	MLB	20	251	20	7	0	9	28	6	81	0	0	.178/.198/.318

Breakout: 8% Improve: 10% Collapse: 0% Attrition: 3% MLB: 10%
Comparables: Matt Davidson, Rafael Devers, Ryan McMahon

If you wanted to design a third base prospect starter set, Potts would make an effective model. San Diego's first-round pick in 2016 is a good athlete who lacks the lateral range required to play up the middle. He's not slow, but you wouldn't quite call him fast. His above-average arm is more than strong enough for the hot corner. At the plate, he has plenty of raw power but doesn't project to hit for a high average.

As is often the case with these player types, Potts's ultimate role will be shaped by whether he can make enough hard contact to facilitate the power. He's an aggressive hitter prone to expanding the strike zone, and his pitch recognition needs refinement. Provided that he stays healthy, we should learn quite a bit about Potts this season; the Double-A test looms large.

YEAR	TEAM	LVL	AGE	PA	DRC+	VORP	BABIP	BRR	FRAA	WARP
2016	PDR	RK	17	195	131	14.1	.356	1.4	SS(14): -1.1, 3B(4): 0.8	0.4
2016	TRI	A-	17	72	94	5.0	.298	0.8	SS(10): 1.1, 3B(3): -0.2	0.2
2017	FTW	A	18	522	91	9.8	.312	-0.5	3B(116): -6.9, SS(2): 0.2	-0.3
2018	LEL	A+	19	453	145	36.6	.348	0.3	3B(99): 0.7, 1B(8): 0.1	2.4
2018	SAN	AA	19	89	43	-2.9	.233	-0.2	3B(21): 0.3	-0.4
2019	SDN	MLB	20	251	33	-15.0	.221	-0.5	3B -1, 1B 0	-1.7

Boog Powell OF

Born: 01/14/93 Age: 26 Bats: L Throws: L
Height: 5'10" Weight: 185 Origin: Round 20, 2012 Draft (#619 overall)

YEAR	TEAM	LVL	AGE	PA	R	2B	3B	HR	RBI	BB	K	SB	CS	AVG/OBP/SLG
2016	TAC	AAA	23	277	39	9	2	3	27	22	42	10	6	.270/.326/.359
2017	SEA	MLB	24	43	6	0	0	0	2	6	9	0	0	.194/.310/.194
2017	TAC	AAA	24	239	46	9	2	6	33	28	27	11	5	.340/.416/.490
2017	OAK	MLB	24	92	18	5	0	3	10	9	21	0	1	.321/.380/.494
2018	OAK	MLB	25	25	3	1	1	0	0	1	6	1	1	.167/.200/.292
2018	NAS	AAA	25	174	18	2	0	0	8	23	36	5	6	.224/.333/.238
2019	SDN	MLB	26	251	29	6	1	5	20	23	58	5	4	.212/.290/.309

Breakout: 6% Improve: 39% Collapse: 9% Attrition: 23% MLB: 69%
Comparables: Bryan Petersen, Charlie Blackmon, Trevor Crowe

Powell began 2018 as the A's starting center fielder, but then sprained his knee, sprained his thumb while on a rehab assignment for the knee and got outrighted off the 40-man roster rather than called up when rosters expanded. He's still just 26, so if you write off 2018 as a lost season and start 2019 with a blank slate, there's still room for mild optimism; a second-division starter in center, with surprising pop for his size and enough athleticism to handle the position, is not out of the question.

YEAR	TEAM	LVL	AGE	PA	DRC+	VORP	BABIP	BRR	FRAA	WARP
2016	TAC	AAA	23	277	79	5.8	.311	0.5	CF(61): 1.4	0.0
2017	SEA	MLB	24	43	91	-1.1	.259	0.0	LF(8): 0.7, RF(1): 0.0	0.1
2017	TAC	AAA	24	239	133	23.3	.364	0.9	RF(25): -0.9, CF(24): -1.7	1.0
2017	OAK	MLB	24	92	94	8.9	.390	1.7	CF(28): 2.0	0.6
2018	OAK	MLB	25	25	67	-2.0	.222	-0.2	CF(7): -1.6	-0.2
2018	NAS	AAA	25	174	64	-3.2	.297	-0.3	RF(21): 1.1, CF(14): 3.4	-0.1
2019	SDN	MLB	26	251	67	-1.9	.262	-0.4	CF 0, RF 0	-0.2

Buddy Reed CF

Born: 04/27/95 Age: 24 Bats: B Throws: R
Height: 6'4" Weight: 210 Origin: Round 2, 2016 Draft (#48 overall)

YEAR	TEAM	LVL	AGE	PA	R	2B	3B	HR	RBI	BB	K	SB	CS	AVG/OBP/SLG
2016	TRI	A-	21	231	31	9	4	0	13	22	53	15	5	.254/.326/.337
2017	FTW	A	22	347	48	17	8	6	35	23	97	12	8	.234/.290/.396
2018	LEL	A+	23	343	54	21	7	12	47	24	84	33	7	.324/.371/.549
2018	SAN	AA	23	195	21	7	0	1	15	12	63	18	3	.179/.227/.235
2019	*SDN*	*MLB*	*24*	*251*	*30*	*7*	*1*	*6*	*19*	*10*	*83*	*11*	*3*	*.168/.198/.289*

Breakout: 1% Improve: 1% Collapse: 0% Attrition: 1% MLB: 1%
Comparables: Noel Cuevas, Paulo Orlando, Jared Hoying

Nobody doubts Reed's speed or ability to run 'em down in center, but scouts have long questioned whether his stiff and slappy swing would ultimately limit his upside. After a year-and-a-half of modest production, Reed finally hit a little bit last year, posting career highs across the board and earning a trip to the Futures Game for his efforts. It should take more than a sky-high BABIP and uncharacteristic power in the Cal League, however, before Padres fans get excited. Double-A arms carved Reed up after a late-season promotion, and the guess here is that he'll plateau as a defensive-minded fourth outfielder.

YEAR	TEAM	LVL	AGE	PA	DRC+	VORP	BABIP	BRR	FRAA	WARP
2016	TRI	A-	21	231	88	8.3	.338	3.5	CF(50): 3.9	0.4
2017	FTW	A	22	347	81	6.1	.315	1.1	CF(85): 1.0	0.1
2018	LEL	A+	23	343	137	39.6	.407	6.5	LF(54): -6.1, CF(15): 1.8	1.4
2018	SAN	AA	23	195	19	-9.0	.263	2.6	CF(39): 8.1, LF(3): 0.5	-0.3
2019	*SDN*	*MLB*	*24*	*251*	*22*	*-13.6*	*.220*	*1.9*	*LF -1, CF 2*	*-1.3*

Esteury Ruiz 2B
Born: 02/15/99 Age: 20 Bats: R Throws: R
Height: 6'0" Weight: 169 Origin: International Free Agent, 2015

YEAR	TEAM	LVL	AGE	PA	R	2B	3B	HR	RBI	BB	K	SB	CS	AVG/OBP/SLG
2016	DRY	RK	17	244	44	18	5	5	26	19	35	13	10	.313/.378/.512
2017	ROY	RK	18	91	22	10	6	3	23	4	20	9	0	.419/.440/.779
2017	PDR	RK	18	134	23	10	4	1	16	9	34	17	6	.300/.364/.475
2018	FTW	A	19	493	63	20	5	12	53	38	141	49	11	.253/.324/.403
2019	SDN	MLB	20	251	29	12	2	7	20	5	84	9	2	.178/.191/.326

Breakout: 10% Improve: 10% Collapse: 0% Attrition: 6% MLB: 10%
Comparables: Dilson Herrera, Nick Noonan, Renato Nunez

For the first time in his life, Ruiz struggled on the baseball field. "Struggle" is a relative word here: As a 19-year-old amid his first taste of full-season ball—and presumably first exposure to April in the Midwest—he was an above-average hitter, and his 49 steals paced the circuit. After dominating the complex leagues, though, Ruiz's 2018 campaign was a small step back. He struck out in nearly 30 percent of his plate appearances and chased far too many pitches out of the zone, undercutting his above-average raw power. He also did little to assuage concerns that he'll slip down the defensive spectrum. We're not big fans of fielding percentage at Baseball Prospectus, but any time you flirt with .900, things can't be going well. Ruiz's power-speed combo can still work if he has to transition from the keystone to left field, but there's much more pressure on his bat out there, and it's fair to speculate that his grip-N-rip approach will leave him too exposed against upper-level arms for the profile to actualize.

YEAR	TEAM	LVL	AGE	PA	DRC+	VORP	BABIP	BRR	FRAA	WARP
2016	DRY	RK	17	244	154	31.2	.354	2.2	2B(23): -0.8, SS(9): -1.8	1.5
2017	ROY	RK	18	91	196	22.3	.516	3.3	2B(17): 3.8	1.2
2017	PDR	RK	18	134	197	11.9	.412	1.8	2B(28): -0.9	0.9
2018	FTW	A	19	493	96	21.3	.345	5.8	2B(74): -1.2, 3B(16): -2.6	0.6
2019	SDN	MLB	20	251	34	-10.3	.235	1.9	2B 0, 3B -1	-1.2

Chris Stewart C

Born: 02/19/82 Age: 37 Bats: R Throws: R
Height: 6'4" Weight: 215 Origin: Round 12, 2001 Draft (#373 overall)

YEAR	TEAM	LVL	AGE	PA	R	2B	3B	HR	RBI	BB	K	SB	CS	AVG/OBP/SLG
2016	PIT	MLB	34	113	10	4	0	1	7	12	15	0	0	.214/.319/.286
2017	PIT	MLB	35	144	8	1	2	0	4	9	22	0	0	.183/.241/.221
2018	ATL	MLB	36	16	3	0	0	0	3	1	1	0	0	.214/.250/.214
2018	GWN	AAA	36	156	17	6	1	0	10	14	17	0	1	.219/.299/.277
2018	ARI	MLB	36	1	0	0	0	0	0	0	0	0	0	.000/.000/.000
2019	SDN	MLB	37	32	3	1	0	1	3	3	6	0	0	.207/.281/.345

Breakout: 3% Improve: 34% Collapse: 5% Attrition: 10% MLB: 64%
Comparables: Ryan Hanigan, Brad Ausmus, Bob Boone

You have no idea why you keep it around. Who are you kidding? You're not actually going to use that blender you got as a wedding gift all those years ago. You've used it, what, a handful of times over the last couple of years because you felt guilty? You're not a smoothie person and you prefer your margaritas on the rocks anyway. But what if you really did need it and didn't have it? Could you live without it? Probably, but if the in-laws show up and that thing isn't still taking up counter space you'd catch hell. And who knows — you might just need it one day after all. Best to hold onto that blender just in case. It does, technically, still work.

YEAR	TEAM	P. COUNT	FRM RUNS	BLK RUNS	THRW RUNS	TOT RUNS
2016	PIT	4077	-0.8	-1.5	0.0	-2.6
2017	PIT	5872	2.3	0.6	0.1	2.6
2018	ATL	632	-0.3	0.0	0.0	0.1
2018	GWN	6076	-1.7	-0.3	0.1	-1.7
2018	ARI	57	0.0	0.0	0.0	-0.6
2019	SDN	1238	-0.3	-0.1	0.0	-0.5

YEAR	TEAM	LVL	AGE	PA	DRC+	VORP	BABIP	BRR	FRAA	WARP
2016	PIT	MLB	34	113	88	2.9	.244	0.6	C(31): -2.9, 1B(1): 0.0	0.1
2017	PIT	MLB	35	144	69	-6.0	.220	0.0	C(48): 3.3	0.5
2018	ATL	MLB	36	16	94	0.3	.214	0.6	C(5): -0.4	0.1
2018	GWN	AAA	36	156	69	0.1	.248	-0.3	C(45): -1.4	-0.2
2018	ARI	MLB	36	1	91	-0.1	.000	0.0	C(3): 0.0	0.0
2019	SDN	MLB	37	32	83	0.9	.257	-0.1	C -1	0.0

San Diego Padres 2019

Fernando Tatis Jr. SS
Born: 01/02/99 Age: 20 Bats: R Throws: R
Height: 6'3" Weight: 185 Origin: International Free Agent, 2015

YEAR	TEAM	LVL	AGE	PA	R	2B	3B	HR	RBI	BB	K	SB	CS	AVG/OBP/SLG
2016	PDR	RK	17	188	35	13	1	4	20	10	44	14	2	.273/.312/.426
2016	TRI	A-	17	49	4	4	2	0	5	3	13	1	1	.273/.306/.455
2017	FTW	A	18	518	78	26	7	21	69	75	124	29	15	.281/.390/.520
2017	SAN	AA	18	57	6	1	0	1	6	2	17	3	0	.255/.281/.327
2018	SAN	AA	19	394	77	22	4	16	43	33	109	16	5	.286/.355/.507
2019	SDN	MLB	20	284	33	11	1	11	32	14	91	6	2	.199/.240/.372

Breakout: 15% Improve: 32% Collapse: 0% Attrition: 16% MLB: 32%
Comparables: Xander Bogaerts, Addison Russell, Cody Bellinger

It's almost inconceivable that, less than three years ago, the Padres were able to acquire Tatis in exchange for James Shields (that the White Sox absorbed nearly $30 million is a hilarious footnote). Now entering his age-20 season, Fernando the Younger is the crown jewel in San Diego's sterling collection of young talent. Scouts project that he'll be a .270 hitter who can bash 25 homers per year in his prime, with room for more if his pitch recognition and plate discipline improve. If Tatis were a first baseman, he'd be an interesting prospect. As a shortstop? Well, he's one of the two or three best in the game.

It's worth mentioning that, for a top prospect, the delta of outcomes here is quite large. Tatis is young, super athletic and toolsy, which suggests that he has room to grow. But his youth also means that his track record isn't real long, and he hasn't faced many elite pitchers; we don't know how big leaguers will be able to exploit the one weakness in his game (plate discipline). There's a world where Tatis turns into a third basemen with contact issues that sap some of the power everyone expects out of him, like the best version of his father. But there's also a future where Tatis stays at short, works better counts and adds strength without sacrificing athleticism. That guy is a superstar, and the kind of franchise player you can build a team around. We won't know where Tatis fits along that spectrum for a few years, but Padres fans may get their first look at him as soon as this summer.

YEAR	TEAM	LVL	AGE	PA	DRC+	VORP	BABIP	BRR	FRAA	WARP
2016	PDR	RK	17	188	117	13.0	.344	2.4	SS(29): -0.1, 2B(8): -1.3	0.3
2016	TRI	A-	17	49	110	4.5	.364	0.4	SS(7): -1.4, 3B(3): -0.7	-0.2
2017	FTW	A	18	518	150	51.2	.342	0.1	SS(109): -5.6	3.7
2017	SAN	AA	18	57	75	0.4	.351	0.9	SS(9): -0.3, 3B(3): -0.5	-0.1
2018	SAN	AA	19	394	136	35.8	.370	3.0	SS(83): -1.9	2.4
2019	SDN	MLB	20	284	60	-2.0	.253	0.6	SS -1	-0.5

Luis Urias 2B

Born: 06/03/97 Age: 22 Bats: R Throws: R
Height: 5'9" Weight: 185 Origin: International Free Agent, 2013

YEAR	TEAM	LVL	AGE	PA	R	2B	3B	HR	RBI	BB	K	SB	CS	AVG/OBP/SLG
2016	LEL	A+	19	531	71	26	5	5	52	40	36	7	13	.330/.397/.440
2017	SAN	AA	20	526	77	20	4	3	38	68	65	7	5	.296/.398/.380
2018	ELP	AAA	21	533	83	30	7	8	45	67	109	2	1	.296/.398/.447
2018	SDN	MLB	21	53	5	1	0	2	5	3	10	1	0	.208/.264/.354
2019	SDN	MLB	22	396	41	15	3	9	42	40	86	1	1	.241/.328/.380

Breakout: 20% Improve: 48% Collapse: 0% Attrition: 27% MLB: 53%
Comparables: Kolten Wong, J.P. Crawford, Steve Lombardozzi

Another of the cornerstone prospects in San Diego's rebuild, Urias is a high-floor second baseman. He's a good defender at the keystone—he can handle short in a pinch—but it's his bat that carries the profile. His athleticism, bat speed and feel for contact portends a future as a .300 hitter; his short frame and high leg kick suggests he could do so in style. He'll need to hit for average to have value, and most scouts think he's up to the task. The big question is whether there's juice in the profile beyond that.

Between a lively ball and the launch angle revolution, we've seen a much wider range of outcomes from the "good hit, low power" profile in recent years. Some players have been able to add loft to their swings, and combine excellent hand/eye coordination with their new bat path to unlock previously untapped power; others never get the hang of the new mechanics and take a step back. It's too early to tell where Urias will fit on this elongated spectrum, and it's not fair to project an attribute he's scarcely shown in the minors. Whether any power comes or not, Urias should play good D and get on base quite a bit. All that this is meant to say is that he's very likely to be a productive player, and that there's also a glimmer of star potential.

YEAR	TEAM	LVL	AGE	PA	DRC+	VORP	BABIP	BRR	FRAA	WARP
2016	LEL	A+	19	531	148	41.6	.348	-5.9	2B(80): 6.2, SS(22): -3.2	2.5
2017	SAN	AA	20	526	130	40.3	.340	2.6	SS(60): 4.7, 2B(55): -1.1	3.0
2018	ELP	AAA	21	533	117	27.3	.373	1.4	2B(90): 10.2, SS(20): 3.4	3.7
2018	SDN	MLB	21	53	85	0.6	.216	0.3	2B(12): -0.2	0.1
2019	SDN	MLB	22	396	92	11.1	.291	-0.4	2B 3, SS 0	1.4

Logan Allen LHP

Born: 05/23/97   Age: 22   Bats: R   Throws: L
Height: 6'3"   Weight: 200   Origin: Round 8, 2015 Draft (#231 overall)

YEAR	TEAM	LVL	AGE	W	L	SV	G	GS	IP	H	HR	BB/9	K/9	K	GB%	BABIP
2016	FTW	A	19	3	4	0	15	11	54	48	2	3.7	7.8	47	38%	.301
2017	FTW	A	20	5	4	0	13	13	68^1	49	1	3.4	11.2	85	43%	.294
2017	LEL	A+	20	2	5	0	11	10	56^2	60	2	2.9	9.1	57	50%	.352
2018	SAN	AA	21	10	6	0	20	19	121	89	7	2.8	9.3	125	43%	.269
2018	ELP	AAA	21	4	0	0	5	5	27^2	21	4	4.2	8.5	26	38%	.236
2019	SDN	MLB	22	1	1	0	3	3	15	14	2	3.8	8.7	15	39%	.293

Breakout: 10%   Improve: 19%   Collapse: 10%   Attrition: 18%   MLB: 43%
Comparables: Mike Montgomery, Giovanni Soto, Josh Hader

Allen's five-word scouting report is "lefty with a plus change," a description that implies an undersized, crafty southpaw getting by on guile rather than velocity. But Allen defies the stereotype. Listed at 6-foot-3 and 200 pounds, Allen can rush his fastball into the mid-90s and his command is actually one of the weaker attributes in the profile. Still, most evaluators project an average grade in that department at maturity, which makes him a strike-thrower without pinpoint accuracy. Between all that and an average curveball, Allen has the ingredients to be a mid-rotation starter, the kind who always seems to be pitching the day you decide to go the park.

YEAR	TEAM	LVL	AGE	WHIP	ERA	DRA	WARP	MPH	FB%	WHF	CSP
2016	FTW	A	19	1.30	3.33	3.85	0.7				
2017	FTW	A	20	1.10	2.11	3.86	1.1				
2017	LEL	A+	20	1.38	3.97	3.84	0.9				
2018	SAN	AA	21	1.05	2.75	3.35	2.8				
2018	ELP	AAA	21	1.23	1.63	6.12	-0.2				
2019	SDN	MLB	22	1.34	4.26	4.56	0.1				

Michel Baez RHP

Born: 01/21/96   Age: 23   Bats: R   Throws: R
Height: 6'8"   Weight: 220   Origin: International Free Agent, 2016

YEAR	TEAM	LVL	AGE	W	L	SV	G	GS	IP	H	HR	BB/9	K/9	K	GB%	BABIP
2017	FTW	A	21	6	2	0	10	10	58²	41	8	1.2	12.6	82	36%	.264
2018	LEL	A+	22	4	7	0	17	17	86²	73	5	3.4	9.6	92	37%	.297
2018	SAN	AA	22	0	3	0	4	4	18¹	22	4	5.9	10.3	21	31%	.375
2019	SDN	MLB	23	5	6	0	16	16	83²	81	14	3.7	9.4	87	34%	.313

Breakout: 9%   Improve: 16%   Collapse: 14%   Attrition: 28%   MLB: 41%
Comparables: Aaron Blair, Jon Gray, Jake Odorizzi

On BP's top 10 prospect list for San Diego, Wilson Karman aptly likened Baez's appearance to "a cardboard cutout of Dellin Betances." Blessed with all of the height and none of the girth of the Yankees fireballer, Baez is an interesting arm in his own right. He reaches the upper 90s with his fastball and complements the pitch with a tumbling change that plays up because of the unusually high angle he throws from. He also works with two breaking balls, and the slider in particular looks like a potential bat-misser.

But Baez's stature is a mixed blessing. While there isn't a magic line separating pitchers taller and shorter than six-and-a-half feet, that height is a tipping point at which the taller pitchers almost universally struggle with repeating their mechanics. It's just much harder for a 6-foot-8 pitcher to marshal his limbs toward the plate than it is for someone shorter. While he repeats his motion pretty well for a giant, things get ugly when he's out of sync, and it happens often enough to give evaluators pause. Baez is a very promising young arm, but there's a lot of reliever risk in the profile.

YEAR	TEAM	LVL	AGE	WHIP	ERA	DRA	WARP	MPH	FB%	WHF	CSP
2017	FTW	A	21	0.84	2.45	2.60	1.8				
2018	LEL	A+	22	1.22	2.91	4.01	1.3				
2018	SAN	AA	22	1.85	7.36	3.22	0.5				
2019	SDN	MLB	23	1.38	4.67	5.20	0.1				

San Diego Padres 2019

Anderson Espinoza   RHP
Born: 03/09/98   Age: 21   Bats: R   Throws: R
Height: 6'0"   Weight: 160   Origin: International Free Agent, 2014

YEAR	TEAM	LVL	AGE	W	L	SV	G	GS	IP	H	HR	BB/9	K/9	K	GB%	BABIP
2016	GRN	A	18	5	8	0	17	17	76	77	2	3.2	8.5	72	49%	.342
2016	FTW	A	18	1	3	0	8	7	32^1	38	1	2.2	7.8	28	44%	.363
2019	SDN	MLB	21	2	3	0	8	8	34	38	5	3.9	7.1	27	41%	.325

Breakout: 3%   Improve: 3%   Collapse: 1%   Attrition: 3%   MLB: 6%
Comparables: Taylor Guerrieri, Tyler Clippard, Alex Sanabia

The enigma of San Diego's talented farm system, Espinoza has started only seven minor-league games since arriving in 2016's Drew Pomeranz deal. Elbow discomfort in early 2017 begat Tommy John surgery that August, and the recovery process effectively sidelined him for two full years. That's a blow for someone like Espinoza, who has enticing tools but little feel for using them. It's possible that he comes back fully intact, looking like a future No. 2 starter and throwing 95-97 while flashing a plus curve and changeup. He's still only 21, and if he's in the Cal League this summer, he'll be ahead of schedule. But with all the missed reps, a bit of rust seems inevitable. A healthy season would do him a world of good but even if he manages to start 25 games, we'll learn more about him in 2020 than 2019.

YEAR	TEAM	LVL	AGE	WHIP	ERA	DRA	WARP	MPH	FB%	WHF	CSP
2016	GRN	A	18	1.37	4.38	3.71	1.2				
2016	FTW	A	18	1.42	4.73	3.84	0.5				
2019	SDN	MLB	21	1.54	4.94	5.51	-0.1				

MacKenzie Gore LHP

Born: 02/24/99 Age: 20 Bats: L Throws: L
Height: 6'3" Weight: 191 Origin: Round 1, 2017 Draft (#3 overall)

YEAR	TEAM	LVL	AGE	W	L	SV	G	GS	IP	H	HR	BB/9	K/9	K	GB%	BABIP
2017	PDR	RK	18	0	1	0	7	7	21¹	14	0	3.0	14.3	34	69%	.333
2018	FTW	A	19	2	5	0	16	16	60²	61	5	2.7	11.0	74	41%	.354
2019	SDN	MLB	20	3	4	0	12	12	45¹	45	8	4.3	9.6	49	45%	.323

Breakout: 5% Improve: 7% Collapse: 1% Attrition: 3% MLB: 10%
Comparables: Henry Owens, Matt Wisler, Michael Fulmer

Several hurlers have a case to be San Diego's top pitching prospect, but Gore is our pick here at BP. He's just two years removed from high school ball and already flashing four above average pitches with plus command. Headlined by a sinking fastball that touches 96 and a fading change, Gore is advanced for his age. Still, there are risks. He's already battling recurring blister issues, he's never pitched above A-ball, and from all photographic evidence, his next shave will be his first. Still, he throws hard, knows where it's going and has multiple secondaries to miss a bat with. This is what a No. 2 starter looks like at 19-years-old.

YEAR	TEAM	LVL	AGE	WHIP	ERA	DRA	WARP	MPH	FB%	WHF	CSP
2017	PDR	RK	18	0.98	1.27	2.99	0.7				
2018	FTW	A	19	1.30	4.45	2.81	1.7				
2019	SDN	MLB	20	1.47	4.83	5.39	0.0				

Adrian Morejon   LHP

Born: 02/27/99   Age: 20   Bats: L   Throws: L
Height: 6'0"   Weight: 175   Origin: International Free Agent, 2016

YEAR	TEAM	LVL	AGE	W	L	SV	G	GS	IP	H	HR	BB/9	K/9	K	GB%	BABIP
2017	TRI	A-	18	2	2	0	7	7	35^1	37	2	0.8	8.9	35	41%	.337
2017	FTW	A	18	1	2	0	6	6	27^2	28	2	4.2	7.5	23	34%	.321
2018	LEL	A+	19	4	4	0	13	13	62^2	54	6	3.4	10.1	70	55%	.302
2019	SDN	MLB	20	3	4	0	12	12	55^2	54	7	3.9	8.7	54	42%	.316

Breakout: 2%   Improve: 2%   Collapse: 0%   Attrition: 2%   MLB: 3%
Comparables: Casey Kelly, Brad Keller, Jeurys Familia

Morejon's prospect profile hasn't changed much since San Diego signed him three years ago. The Cuban still works into the mid-90s with a biting two-plane curve. He's still succeeding against much older competition, still earning plaudits for his pitchability and command. He's still undersized and still working on that changeup.

There are positives and negatives to this sort of continuity. On the plus side, he remains on track to reach San Diego in his early-20s. But one big reason why Morejon appeared prominently on top prospect lists throughout his career was because he was so advanced so young, which gave him ample developmental time to iron out the wrinkles. That hasn't happened—at least not to the degree required to become one of baseball's very best pitching prospects. The change still looks fringy, his arm strength never took a step forward and the concerns evaluators raised about his small frame have manifested as well, first with a missed start here and there and then with his first trip to the disabled list in 2018. This probably reads more negatively than it should. Morejon still has every chance of becoming a good big league starter. He is, however, perhaps less likely to be a great one than he was this time two years ago.

YEAR	TEAM	LVL	AGE	WHIP	ERA	DRA	WARP	MPH	FB%	WHF	CSP
2017	TRI	A-	18	1.13	3.57	3.94	0.6				
2017	FTW	A	18	1.48	4.23	4.83	0.1				
2018	LEL	A+	19	1.24	3.30	3.86	1.1				
2019	SDN	MLB	20	1.40	4.31	4.80	0.3				

Chris Paddack   RHP

Born: 01/08/96   Age: 23   Bats: R   Throws: R
Height: 6'4"   Weight: 195   Origin: Round 8, 2015 Draft (#236 overall)

YEAR	TEAM	LVL	AGE	W	L	SV	G	GS	IP	H	HR	BB/9	K/9	K	GB%	BABIP
2016	GRB	A	20	2	0	0	6	6	28^1	9	2	0.6	15.2	48	51%	.163
2016	FTW	A	20	0	0	0	3	3	14	11	0	1.9	14.8	23	45%	.379
2018	LEL	A+	22	4	1	0	10	10	52^1	43	3	0.7	14.3	83	47%	.370
2018	SAN	AA	22	3	2	0	7	7	37^2	23	1	1.0	8.8	37	45%	.239
2019	SDN	MLB	23	2	1	0	5	5	25	21	3	2.4	10.7	30	42%	.294

Breakout: 12%   Improve: 29%   Collapse: 13%   Attrition: 19%   MLB: 49%
Comparables: Drew Smyly, David Paulino, Marcus Stroman

As a prospect, Paddack is mature beyond his years, like a teen who finishes his homework early and still gets to go out on the weekends. He has better control than just about any other prospect in baseball, and he didn't miss a beat after returning from Tommy John surgery. In 90 innings across two levels, he posted an absurd 15:1 strikeout-to-walk ratio while allowing only four homers. Given that he spent most of the season in the hitter-friendly California League, those numbers are all the more impressive. At 92-94 mph, Paddack won't blow anyone away but he's not a soft-tosser either, and the changeup is his bread and butter anyway. The change features late, tumbling action, and he throws it while maintaining the same arm speed as his fastball. It gives everyone fits, and could help Paddack shine as a mid-rotation starter as soon as 2019.

YEAR	TEAM	LVL	AGE	WHIP	ERA	DRA	WARP	MPH	FB%	WHF	CSP
2016	GRB	A	20	0.39	0.95	0.89	1.4				
2016	FTW	A	20	1.00	0.64	2.51	0.4				
2018	LEL	A+	22	0.90	2.24	2.40	1.8				
2018	SAN	AA	22	0.72	1.91	2.87	1.1				
2019	SDN	MLB	23	1.10	3.15	3.38	0.5				

San Diego Padres 2019

Luis Patino RHP
Born: 10/26/99   Age: 19   Bats: R   Throws: R
Height: 6'0"   Weight: 192   Origin: International Free Agent, 2016

YEAR	TEAM	LVL	AGE	W	L	SV	G	GS	IP	H	HR	BB/9	K/9	K	GB%	BABIP
2017	DPA	RK	17	2	1	0	4	4	16	11	0	1.1	8.4	15	58%	.256
2017	PDR	RK	17	2	1	0	9	8	40	32	2	3.6	9.7	43	50%	.286
2018	FTW	A	18	6	3	0	17	17	83^1	65	1	2.6	10.6	98	45%	.320
2019	SDN	MLB	19	3	5	0	13	13	62	61	10	4.3	9.2	63	43%	.318

Breakout: 8%   Improve: 12%   Collapse: 0%   Attrition: 8%   MLB: 12%
Comparables: Madison Bumgarner, Jordan Lyles, Roberto Osuna

Few teams are lucky enough to have an 18-year-old who mixes premium athleticism, a high-90s fastball and a potentially plus breaking ball; only the Padres can credibly claim their system has 10 superior prospects. To be sure, Patino is no sure thing: He needs to develop a third pitch, his mechanics are a little violent for a starter and there's a long way between his present workload and the innings he'll need to eat in a big-league rotation. But even with those developmental hurdles ahead, he's one of the real sleepers in all of baseball. Patino is as projectable as they come, and don't be surprised if his prospect stock soars in 2019.

YEAR	TEAM	LVL	AGE	WHIP	ERA	DRA	WARP	MPH	FB%	WHF	CSP
2017	DPA	RK	17	0.81	1.69	3.72	0.4				
2017	PDR	RK	17	1.20	2.47	3.35	1.1				
2018	FTW	A	18	1.07	2.16	3.53	1.6				
2019	SDN	MLB	19	1.46	4.83	5.38	0.0				

Cal Quantrill RHP

Born: 02/10/95   Age: 24   Bats: L   Throws: R
Height: 6'3"   Weight: 208   Origin: Round 1, 2016 Draft (#8 overall)

YEAR	TEAM	LVL	AGE	W	L	SV	G	GS	IP	H	HR	BB/9	K/9	K	GB%	BABIP
2016	PDR	RK	21	0	2	0	5	5	13^2	12	0	1.3	10.5	16	49%	.324
2016	TRI	A-	21	0	2	0	5	5	18^2	15	0	1.0	13.5	28	56%	.333
2017	LEL	A+	22	6	5	0	14	14	73^2	78	5	2.9	9.3	76	42%	.353
2017	SAN	AA	22	1	5	0	8	8	42^1	52	5	3.4	7.2	34	39%	.341
2018	SAN	AA	23	6	5	0	22	22	117	135	12	2.9	7.8	101	45%	.336
2018	ELP	AAA	23	3	1	0	6	6	31	39	4	1.5	6.4	22	50%	.333
2019	SDN	MLB	24	1	1	0	3	3	15	16	2	3.4	8.0	13	42%	.296

Breakout: 11%   Improve: 18%   Collapse: 5%   Attrition: 17%   MLB: 24%
Comparables: Scott Diamond, Sam Howard, Wade Miley

Another year, another season in which Quantrill's prospect stock sagged mildly, like a shirt slowly losing its vibrancy with repeated washings. Once a legitimate 1:1 candidate, Quantrill had Tommy John surgery in 2015, and his stuff never quite made it to the other side. After tossing 150 innings last year, he seems to be healthy, or at least stable, but his pedestrian whiff numbers reflect the degradation of his arsenal. That's not to say he isn't a viable big leaguer: Quantrill can locate his fastball, and the pitch scrapes the mid-90s with quite a bit of movement. His changeup isn't as nasty as it was in college, but both that and his breaking balls are usable secondaries. It all adds up to a perfectly serviceable No. 4 starter. That's nothing to scoff at, even if it isn't quite the career path we envisioned for him three years ago.

YEAR	TEAM	LVL	AGE	WHIP	ERA	DRA	WARP	MPH	FB%	WHF	CSP
2016	PDR	RK	21	1.02	5.27	2.63	0.5				
2016	TRI	A-	21	0.91	1.93	1.69	0.8				
2017	LEL	A+	22	1.38	3.67	3.65	1.4				
2017	SAN	AA	22	1.61	4.04	3.75	0.7				
2018	SAN	AA	23	1.48	5.15	4.18	1.6				
2018	ELP	AAA	23	1.42	3.48	3.97	0.6				
2019	SDN	MLB	24	1.43	4.54	4.86	0.0				

Ryan Weathers LHP

Born: 12/17/99 Age: 19 Bats: L Throws: L
Height: 6'1" Weight: 200 Origin: Round 1, 2018 Draft (#7 overall)

YEAR	TEAM	LVL	AGE	W	L	SV	G	GS	IP	H	HR	BB/9	K/9	K	GB%	BABIP
2018	SDP	RK	18	0	2	0	4	4	9^1	8	2	2.9	8.7	9	69%	.222
2018	FTW	A	18	0	1	0	3	3	9	11	0	1.0	9.0	9	58%	.355
2019	SDN	MLB	19	2	3	0	9	9	33^2	37	5	4.4	7.1	26	50%	.319

Comparables: John Barbato, Jaime Barria, Wilfredo Boscan

Like anxious parents nervously giving a spoiled child bad news, teams tend to baby their first-round pitchers, introducing them to professional baseball slowly. If they pitch at all that first year, they'll get a cushy assignment to the complex leagues or short-season ball, where they'll overmatch hitters far below their talent level. Not so with Weathers. San Diego signed him quickly and he wound up making a few starts at Low-A Fort Wayne, a league that rarely sees a pitcher fresh out of high school.

The aggressive development path speaks to Weathers' maturity on the mound. The son of 19-year big-league vet David Weathers, Weathers the Younger works with a low-to-mid-90s fastball, a power curve, and a changeup that's already above average. He's athletic for a kid his size and he repeats his delivery well. His ceiling may ultimately not be as high as some of the other players taken in the top 10 last year, but for a high school pitcher, he's a pretty safe bet. No junk stock jokes, please.

YEAR	TEAM	LVL	AGE	WHIP	ERA	DRA	WARP	MPH	FB%	WHF	CSP
2018	SDP	RK	18	1.18	3.86	4.59	0.2				
2018	FTW	A	18	1.33	3.00	4.61	0.1				
2019	SDN	MLB	19	1.59	5.36	5.99	-0.3				

LINEOUTS

Hitters

HITTER	POS	TEAM	LVL	AGE	PA	R	2B	3B	HR	RBI	BB	K	SB	CS	AVG/OBP/SLG	DRC+	WARP
Austin Allen	C	SAN	AA	24	498	59	31	0	22	56	37	97	0	3	.290/.351/.506	138	4.0
Gabriel Arias	SS	FTW	A	18	504	54	27	3	6	55	41	149	3	3	.240/.302/.352	85	1.2
Luis Campusano	C	FTW	A	19	284	26	11	0	3	40	19	43	0	1	.288/.345/.365	117	0.8
Allen Cordoba	INF	LEL	A+	22	164	15	6	2	2	16	4	46	3	4	.206/.233/.310	37	-1.2
Allen Craig	1B	ELP	AAA	33	363	52	18	1	13	59	39	73	0	0	.293/.375/.479	120	0.7
Ty France	3B	SAN	AA	23	479	66	22	2	17	77	33	70	3	4	.263/.349/.448	122	0.9
	3B	ELP	AAA	23	110	18	8	0	5	19	13	19	0	0	.287/.382/.532	131	0.9
Greg Garcia	PH	SLN	MLB	28	208	15	6	0	3	15	20	37	3	1	.221/.309/.304	81	0.4
Javier Guerra	SS	ELP	AAA	22	464	52	18	9	13	55	27	166	2	0	.223/.269/.398	43	-2.1
	SS	SDN	MLB	22	19	2	0	0	0	1	3	9	0	0	.125/.263/.125	53	-0.1
Edward Olivares	CF	LEL	A+	22	575	79	25	10	12	62	29	102	21	8	.277/.321/.429	104	1.1
Tirso Ornelas	RF	FTW	A	18	355	45	13	3	8	40	40	68	5	1	.252/.341/.392	106	0.5
Jeisson Rosario	CF	FTW	A	18	521	79	17	5	3	34	66	108	18	12	.271/.368/.353	97	1.0
Luis Torrens	C	LEL	A+	22	515	62	36	3	6	73	26	77	1	1	.280/.320/.406	101	0.8

Austin Allen proved that his strong 2018 numbers were no Cal League mirage, essentially replicating that production in Double-A. He's 25 now, though, and he's still a below average receiver without enough stick to project as a first baseman. Sometimes these types keep hitting all the way up, but there are a lot of tweener indicators here. ⓧ A marquee Latin American signing three years ago, **Gabriel Arias** struggled in 2018. He whiffed in nearly 30 percent of his plate appearances without flashing any of his once-coveted offensive tools in the other 70 percent. He was very young for the Midwest League, so there remains a chance everything comes back around against people (closer to) his own age. ⓧ San Diego's second round pick in 2017, **Luis Campusano** is a fringy defender behind the plate who may grow into plus raw power at maturity. A midseason concussion ended his season just when he was getting hot. ⓧ The Padres were chuffed when Rule 5 draftee **Allen Cordoba** batted .208 in surprisingly regular playing time in 2017; they were considerably less so when he hit .206 in the Cal League last summer. ⓧ It's been six years since **Allen Craig** and Everth Cabrera were All-Star teammates, four since their last big league game, and at least two since you've thought about either one of them. ⓧ The summer of 2016 must seem like a decade ago to **Alex Dickerson**. The late-bloomer cracked San Diego's lineup that July and notched surprisingly productive numbers. Injuries knocked him out for all of the past two years though, and given that he'll be 29 in May, he may have missed his opportunity to contribute in San Diego. ⓧ **A.J. Ellis** put together his best season at the plate since 2015 and lost playing time to Austin Hedges

San Diego Padres 2019

and Francisco Mejia down the stretch regardless. He had more job security back when he was Clayton Kershaw's personal catcher. ⚀ It's good to tie France when you're a World Cup underdog or engaged in trench warfare, but it's not great to **Ty France** if you need an impact first base prospect. ⚀ Always light on power and no longer a viable shortstop, **Greg Garcia** has become a bench bat with too little bat and a utility infielder with too little utility. ⚀ Once a consensus top 100 prospect, this once-promising shortstop will go down as baseball's second-most famous **Javy Guerra**. ⚀ A speedy outfielder with projectable power and a chance to stay in center, **Edward Olivares** would be a top prospect in many organizations. For San Diego, he's one of many enticing young talents. To stand out in this crowded pasture, he must prove he can square up advanced arms and hit for more power in games. ⚀ As baseball itself drifts increasingly toward the Three True Outcomes, **Tirso Ornelas** goes against the grain. Still a teenager, the Mexican corner outfielder has a great eye and approach at the plate and a knack for making solid, line drive contact. Expect him to destroy the Cal League and vault up prospect lists accordingly. ⚀ **Jeisson Rosario** has a strange profile. He's wiry to the point of being thin but he has a very projectable hit tool because of his elite hand-eye coordination and feel for contact. While quick, he's not as much of a burner as you'd think from looking at him, so to make good, the most fickle tool of all has to play to potential. ⚀ A member of San Diego's Rule 5 trio of 2017, **Luis Torrens** batted 139 times as a 21-year-old. He's safely back where he belongs, but with so many promising catchers throughout the system, he's almost entirely off the radar now.

Pitchers

PITCHER	TEAM	LVL	AGE	W	L	SV	G	GS	IP	H	HR	BB/9	K/9	K	GB%	WHIP	ERA	DRA	WARP
Reggie Lawson	LEL	A+	20	8	5	0	24	22	117	130	11	3.9	9.0	117	43%	1.55	4.69	5.57	-0.4
Kazuhisa Makita	ELP	AAA	33	1	1	0	24	0	26^1	23	1	3.4	7.5	22	36%	1.25	3.76	4.85	0.1
	SDN	MLB	33	0	1	0	27	0	35	32	7	3.1	9.5	37	24%	1.26	5.40	5.69	-0.3
Andres Munoz	SAN	AA	19	2	1	7	20	0	19	11	0	5.2	9.0	19	55%	1.16	0.95	3.35	0.4
Sammy Solis	SYR	AAA	29	0	0	0	10	0	9^1	5	0	3.9	10.6	11	46%	0.96	1.93	3.68	0.2
	WAS	MLB	29	1	2	0	56	0	39^1	43	7	4.1	10.1	44	50%	1.55	6.41	4.55	0.2
Brad Wieck	SAN	AA	26	1	2	10	27	0	28	20	1	2.6	11.6	36	29%	1.00	1.93	2.62	0.8
	ELP	AAA	26	3	0	2	17	0	18^1	16	2	4.4	16.7	34	50%	1.36	3.44	1.88	0.7
	SDN	MLB	26	0	0	0	5	0	7	3	1	0.0	12.9	10	29%	0.43	1.29	2.68	0.2

Carter Capps is still hopping on his way to the plate—and still getting himself and his manager kicked out of the game once in a blue moon when an umpire decides that his delivery is just too weird to be street legal. Unless (until?) he gets his good fastball back, though, he'll fight these battles in Triple-A. ⚀ The long 2018 Padres season was the perfect time for a young hurler to hone his craft, but **Dinelson Lamet** missed all the fun recuperating from Tommy John surgery. Despite a strong strikeout rate in 2017, Lamet was already showing a lot of reliever traits, and all the time on the shelf certainly hasn't made that outcome any less likely. ⓧ **Reggie Lawson** is a great guy to have as your seventh-best pitching prospect. He's young and athletic enough to dream on better command and an improved changeup. But even if those never come around, he's added velocity as he's grown and his curveball flashes plus, giving him a potent combination if he's forced into relief work. ⓧ Just the third Japanese player to suit up for the Padres, **Kazuhisa Makita** is an odd fit for the roster. He's on a two-year deal, and it's unclear what his role will be on a team with a plethora of younger and better relief options. ⓧ At long last, a Padres pitching prospect with no chance to start. **Andres Munoz** is the only such player who earned a mention in these pages, but as long as you can hit 103 mph and flash a plus slider, you get your name in the paper. ⓧ Throwing 39 1/3 innings while appearing in 56 games is pretty difficult to do, and not in a good way. **Sammy Solis** allowed a .277/.367/.490 slash line, and will need a serious bounce back to find 50 more games. ⓧ Just what the Padres need, another monster in the bullpen. **Brad Wieck** was 26 when he made his debut, but the gargantuan—he's 6-foot-9—lefty made a heck of an impression, striking out 10 without any walks across seven late-season innings.

Padres Prospects

The State of the System:
Their full-slot, top-ten first-round pick from this year's draft is ranked 12th overall. You tell me.

The Top Ten:

1
Fernando Tatis Jr. SS   OFP: 70   Likely: 60   ETA: 2019
Born: 01/02/99   Age: 20   Bats: R   Throws: R   Height: 6'3"   Weight: 185
Origin: International Free Agent, 2015

The Report: Tatis Jr. is a special talent. He has a wiry and lean frame with plenty of room to add muscle, but he already has explosive strength in his hips and wrists. Tatis is a plus athlete with top tier quick-twitch movements and an instinctual feel for how to move his body to generate power with fluid grace.

With the bat, this translates into some of the best physical offensive tools in baseball. He has a feel for getting the barrel on the ball consistently with a swing he innately understands how to adjust to location and velocity. When he's on a pitch, he can do damage to all fields. Tatis generates plus bat speed, has double-plus raw power, and a swing that takes advantage of both to the fullest. If the physical parts of hitting were all that mattered, Tatis would be ready to go right now.

There's still a bit of developmental work ahead, however. Tatis will need more reps to improve his pitch recognition and calm his approach. He generally knows the zone and has the patience to eschew offerings off the plate, but he also looks to deal damage on pitches he should stay away from. That, along with trouble recognizing plus off-speed out of the hand, occasionally leads to an ugly at-bat.

Defensively, Tatis uses his quickness and average foot speed to get to the balls he should at short, and he oughta stick at the position for now. He has good hands, doesn't make too many mental errors, and his plus arm can dig him out of trouble. He should be an average defender for now, but may need to move to third as he gets slower and bigger.

With a plus bat and average defense, Tatis should be an all-star caliber shortstop, with a real chance at superstardom if he can refine his approach.

The Risks: Low. The only significant risk is Jr.'s lack of polish against premier pitching, but he has consistently shown he's capable of making in-season adjustments. Over the course of the Texas League season, Tatis went from flailing at average breaking balls to recognizing above-average stuff and making hard contact or letting it go.

The only other thing worth mentioning is he still has plenty of room to put on muscle, which could slow him down enough to push him over to third, where he should be plus.

Bret Sayre's Fantasy Take: An easy top-five overall dynasty prospect, Tatito can be a true five-category superstar at shortstop and soon. You already know this though. We're truly picking nits when I say that it was a good sign Tatis was a more effective base stealer in 2018 because one of the risks here was that he'd only be a 10-15 steal guy, rather than in the 25-30 range. Heaven forbid he not run enough to supplement what could be a .275 average and 30 homers from a middle infield spot.

2. Luis Urias   IF

OFP: 70   Likely: 60   ETA: Debuted in 2018
Born: 06/03/97   Age: 22   Bats: R   Throws: R   Height: 5'9"   Weight: 185
Origin: International Free Agent, 2013

The Report: We'll start with a mea culpa: The last few prospect list cycles our west coast folks have buzzed around my ear about Urias, and I treated them like a particularly annoying member of the muscomorpha. It's only a hit tool, and is he really gonna hit? What happens if he only hits .270 and pitchers realize he can't hurt them with any sort of power? Yes, he's young, but there's no projection here, he's just small. He's not really a major league shortstop. I swatted them away with every "reasonable" criticism of the profile I had, as it's not one I'm naturally inclined to pound the table for.

I often write that the lifeblood of our prospect lists are the live looks. Naturally we can't see every prospect every year. We'll send our texts or watch video where needed, but then you see a half dozen or so Urias BP swings and "oh… yeah… of course he is going to hit, and also that is at least average raw power, you idiot, next time listen to Wilson."

I wasn't a co-author on the Nathan Report, so I can't tell you if it was the major league balls, but I do know when a dude has that unnatural carry. We've convened a panel earlier this year to discuss the issues with evaluating this profile, and while yes, he's best-suited to second, isn't really a runner, and hasn't hit for anything approaching average power in the minors, so what?

The Risks: Low. He might walk less if pitchers think they can challenge him. He's not gonna offer a ton of athletic/defensive value. We think he's really gonna hit though.

Bret Sayre's Fantasy Take: I am not going to be a popular guy here. Sure, Urias showed *more* power last year, but color me skeptical that he'll be someone you peg for 15 homers in a season even as he matures. The average is great, no question, and he's one of the best bets in the minors to be a .300 hitter, but not too many of you were fawning over Ben Zobrist last year when he put up a realistic Urias line (.305, 9 HR, 3 SB).

3. Francisco Mejia   C

OFP: 70   Likely: 55   ETA: Debuted in 2017
Born: 10/27/95   Age: 23   Bats: B   Throws: R   Height: 5'10"   Weight: 180
Origin: International Free Agent, 2012

The Report: Last spring, my chat queues were filled with questions along the lines of "What's wrong with Francisco Mejia?" Fair queries given his atrocious start, even if it may have been nothing more than the ol' Triple-A-itis. Once fashionistas could start wearing white, Mejia turned back into the potential .300 hitter with pop that you stashed in your dynasty league two years ago. The slash line looked right in the end, and it matched the eye test. I'm still very confident he will hit.

"Catchers are weird." You might be tired of me writing that by now. So here's another construction: Teams are weird about catchers. I encourage the whole prospect team to write these blurbs—and really, their reports in general—in a vacuum. And my projection for Mejia is "major league catcher." Not a plus one by any means, but a perfectly adequate backstop. He has quite a good arm, and his receiving has improved. He's a bit on the slight side, so durability back there is a fair concern, but Cleveland and now San Diego have demurred when opportunities have presented themselves to make Mejia *the guy*.

Catcher is also the position I am least qualified to evaluate. A lot happens behind closed doors. Teams are just going to know more than I am here, and Yan Gomes and Austin Hedges have justifiably better reps with the glove. But then I see someone try to get in Mejia's kitchen, jam him, and watch him still hit it out, and I wonder if we aren't all overthinking this.

The Risks: High. The funny thing is this risk factor literally just comes down to "Do the Padres think he's a catcher or not?" I've generally been higher on Mejia's glove back there than the organizations that employ him, so ¯_(ツ)_/¯.

Bret Sayre's Fantasy Take: There are two very distinct forces at work in trying to rank Mejia in a dynasty context. The first is that he's a catcher and dynasty league catchers are almost always a bad idea. The second is that the position is so bad that Mejia's upside makes you forget about the first force. Yadier Molina was the second-best fantasy catcher and he hit .261 with 20 homers. Mejia is certainly talented enough offensively to do that if he gets the playing time.

4. MacKenzie Gore   LHP

OFP: 70   Likely: 55   ETA: 2021
Born: 02/24/99   Age: 20   Bats: L   Throws: L   Height: 6'3"   Weight: 191
Origin: Round 1, 2017 Draft (#3 overall)

The Report: Gore was periodically sidelined with recurring blister issues throughout 2018. When healthy, he dominated Midwest League hitters with a mid-90s fastball and a knee buckling curve. There are a lot of moving parts to his delivery but he repeats it well and stays balanced and on line. He's athletic, and there's a chance he develops plus command. While he's not the world's hardest thrower, Gore's extreme extension helps the fastball play above its grade. The curveball is already an above-average offering and has the potential to be a true out pitch. It features 1-7 movement with sharp break and Gore has enough confidence to throw it in any count. The other secondaries are still developing but if they become at least average, they will be a nice complement to his top shelf fastball and curve.

The Risks: High. Gore made three trips to the DL during his first full professional season. He has top-shelf ingredients but the blisters could hinder his progress.

Bret Sayre's Fantasy Take: One of my favorite fantasy pitching prospects, Gore pairs stuff and pitchability in a way that shows you a clear path to being an easy SP2. Of course, he is a pitcher and we really don't like pitching prospects in dynasty leagues, but when Ben and I finally shake out our Top 101, don't be surprised to see Gore as one of the top five pitchers gracing that page. He can ride that fastball/curveball combination to 200-plus strikeouts.

5. Chris Paddack   RHP

OFP: 60   Likely: 55   ETA: 2020
Born: 01/08/96   Age: 23   Bats: R   Throws: R   Height: 6'4"   Weight: 195
Origin: Round 8, 2015 Draft (#236 overall)

The Report: A strong, durable frame and easy physicality highlights the basic package for Paddack, a former eighth-rounder and recent Tommy John rehabber. He looked no worse for wear in his first season back from the knife, dominating High-A and holding his own at Double-A on the back of a stellar fastball-changeup combination that he commands with aplomb. The fastball works in the low-90s, up to 95, and he excels at changing eye levels and attacking up with the pitch. Quality extension helps the pitch play up, and with his command, it's a comfortably above-average pitch. He pairs it with an outstanding plus-or-better changeup that tumbles, fades, and cowers consistently out of harm's way. The spin is the least consistent of his offerings at present, though it projects as a solid-average third pitch. How close it gets to that ceiling will determine how far into the middle of a big-league rotation he can rise.

The Risks: Moderate. He's got TJ on his resumé, and three-and-a-half years after he got drafted he hasn't proven that he'll hold up over the long rigor of a full season. The heater's not overpowering and he still needs to develop some consistency with the hook.

Bret Sayre's Fantasy Take: Boy, Paddack sure came back into dynasty consciousness quickly. Don't let the stats fool you; he's pretty unlikely to be more than a solid SP4 in a solid pitcher's park. But he's pretty close to the majors at this point and given his age, the Padres won't hold him down for long in 2019 if there's an opening and he's upright. Don't expect more than 2018 Mike Fiers and you may not be disappointed.

6. Adrian Morejon   LHP

OFP: 60   Likely: 50   ETA: 2021
Born: 02/27/99   Age: 20   Bats: L   Throws: L   Height: 6'0"   Weight: 175
Origin: International Free Agent, 2016

The Report: The precocious Cuban southpaw more than held his own in the unforgiving California League at age 19, showing advanced feel for his craft along the way. Morejon's frame is mature for his age, and so's his approach to pitching. He'll manipulate his three-pitch mix with an advanced ability to change speeds and land secondaries in the zone to get himself back into counts. His fastball velocity took a big step forward this year, and he's now touching 98 and sitting 93-95 on the regular with quality finish. He'll throw an occasional cut on it and sink it down in the zone, and the pitch shows above-average life. A power curve in the low-80s and a mid-80s change both project to above-average, with the former flashing to plus at its best. There's enough baseline fluidity and athleticism to envision his command becoming an asset at maturity, and the ceiling is impressive if it all comes together.

The Risks: Moderate. There are some health question marks here, as his two-year stateside career now includes multiple minor-but-nagging injuries, including a hip issue that sidelined him for a couple weeks over the summer. His delivery is still inconsistent, and he struggles with his timing enough to suggest that he'll always have much better control than command.

Bret Sayre's Fantasy Take: Despite less flashy numbers, I'd take Morejon over Paddack in a dynasty league right now, and I wouldn't look back. There's sneaky SP2 ceiling with Morejon as his combination of advanced stuff (which keeps looking more advanced) with developing command at such an early stage of his professional career is highly impressive. He'll need to stay healthy, but you could say that about anyone, couldn't you?

7. Luis Patino   RHP

OFP: 60   Likely: 50   ETA: 2021
Born: 10/26/99   Age: 19   Bats: R   Throws: R   Height: 6'0"   Weight: 192
Origin: International Free Agent, 2016

The Report: The 18-year-old Patino burst onto the prospect scene this year with a dominant showing in the Midwest League. He pumped mid-90s heat—touching higher—from deceptive, Kershawian mechanics. That, coupled with his ability to spot the pitch at the bottom of the zone or bust it in to righties, would be more than enough on its own to carve up A-ball lineups, but Patino also has advanced off-speed options for his age as well.

His changeup is his best present pitch. Although it can be a bit firm at times, it shows swing-and-miss potential with good tumble. The curve gives him a second potential above-average secondary with consistent 11-5 shape either side of 80 mph. Patino has a developing hard slider as well, although that is more of a work in progress.

Unsurprisingly the Padres were cautious with his development in 2018. He only pitched into the seventh inning once and was hard-capped around 80 pitches an outing. This is now de rigueur for teenage pitching prospects, but it can make projecting and ranking them tricky. We don't know how Patino's stuff will look under a heavier workload.

To compare him with a couple of his talented prospect mates is to recognize the limitations of what we know; we just have more info about Logan Allen and Michel Baez (both good and ill). Allen and Baez both have more traditional pitcher frames—although Patino could certainly add an inch or two and should get stronger in his twenties. The delta here is just going to be higher. Less of a fallback, but more upside, despite the same role grades.

I'm guessing we are looking at a 10 or 15 spot spread on the 101. This order can be argued a number of different ways, but Patino gets the nod for me in the final published version, because once we (hopefully) fill in some of the missing info on him, the upside here could be special.

The Risks: High. Limited pro track record, and given his smaller size, I would like to see him get a 25 start, 150 IP season under his belt.

Bret Sayre's Fantasy Take: One of the most popular pop-up dynasty prospects during 2018, Patino was extremely impressive not just for his age but, like, for the Earth in Low-A. His youth just adds to both his excitement and risk, but the latter is ultimately likely to leave him as just a really interesting top-150 dynasty prospect to watch rather than someone Ben and I juice up the back half of the 101. What would get him on the 101, you say? A bat, for starters.

8   **Logan Allen   LHP**   OFP: 60   Likely: 50   ETA: 2019
Born: 05/23/97   Age: 22   Bats: R   Throws: L   Height: 6'3"   Weight: 200
Origin: Round 8, 2015 Draft (#231 overall)

The Report: Allen dominated in difficult pitching environments in the upper minors in 2018. He won't blow you away with his stuff like some of the other Padres prospects, and he has the least gaudy radar gun readings among the arms in this Top 10. Allen's fastball sits a couple ticks either side of 90, but there's enough cut to keep it off barrels and the deception in his delivery makes it sneaky fast at times. The delivery has a bit of lefty funk which has impacted his ability to throw strikes at times, but he'll also show you outings where he's pumping the bottom of the zone to both sides.

The major difference maker for him in 2018 has been the development of his slider, which he manipulates between cutter action with deceptive late depth and a more traditional two-plane breaker. It tunnels off the fastball well and could be the bat-misser that he previously lacked. Allen also has a high-70s curve that he struggles to wrangle into a consistent shape and a change he uses sparingly.

The Risks: Medium. Allen dispatched his upper minors assignments without issue, but has had vague elbow problems in the past and it's not exactly plus stuff across the board here.

Bret Sayre's Fantasy Take: Yay, more pitchers. This is nothing against Allen, who's a borderline Top 101 candidate (an impressive feat for a mound dweller), but there are at least 3-4 hitters that I won't get to write fantasy blurbs about who I'd rather own in just about any format. Again, it's a realistic SP4 future without the kind of strikeout numbers to bring him higher. Did you love the 2018 version of Marco Gonzales? Of course you did. What kind of question is that?

9. Michel Baez   RHP

OFP: 60   Likely: 50   ETA: 2020
Born: 01/21/96   Age: 23   Bats: R   Throws: R   Height: 6'8"   Weight: 220
Origin: International Free Agent, 2016

The Report: Baez looks like a cardboard cutout of Dellin Betances; he stands a comparable 6-foot-8 with broad shoulders, but without the same supporting width through his hips and lower half. He leverages that height to generate outstanding plane from an unusual angle, and the combination of a fastball that'll tickle 96 and a tumbling change from on high can give hitters fits when he's consistent through his progressions to slot. He'll work two variants of spin into the mix as well, with a tight slider in the low-80s that'll flash two-plane action and decent bite, along with a mid-70s curve that teases with solid finish and dropping action. The former shows more promise to develop into a solid-average chaser, although there are at present just as many gutters as strikes with both offerings.

The Risks: The above "when he's consistent" disclaimer is a big "if," however. While he indeed flashed better-than-most ability to repeat, the sheer length of his delivery combined with a top-heavy frame lead to periodic struggles maintaining balance and timing through his delivery. There's reliever risk here if his command never comes together, though his stuff and mound presence would make him an excellent option to emerge from a swinging bullpen gate if it comes to that.

Bret Sayre's Fantasy Take: For me, Baez is the clear outlier among the pitchers on this list in that he might not be a top-200 dynasty prospect at this point. It's not really a knock against the stuff, which as you read is more than enough. It's that the odds of him being a starting pitcher are notably lower. If he makes it, he could be a 2008 xFIP superstar, but no one actually projects those pitchers to catch lightning anymore.

10

Hudson Potts   3B   OFP: 55   Likely: 45   ETA: 2020
Born: 10/28/98   Age: 20   Bats: R   Throws: R   Height: 6'3"   Weight: 205
Origin: Round 1, 2016 Draft (#24 overall)

The Report: The 24th overall pick back in 2016, Potts is another youngin' who acquitted himself quite well in High-A—while playing the whole year at the age of a sophomore in college. His glove at the hot corner was arguably the Cal League's best, as he combines soft hands, solid agility, and a nose for angles and hop trajectory to play himself into good defensive position on most balls. His above-average arm strength holds from multiple throwing positions, and he's smooth and true with his transfers on tough plays. There's a good bit of thunder in his stick as well, and he shows a solid baseline command of the strike zone. While his swing was relatively flat and compact this year, he'll take his lift-and-separate hacks in turn, and there's reason to think he could hit for more power than he's shown down the line.

The Risks: As one might expect of a hitter so young for his level, his approach is still nascent, and there were plenty of at-bats this season where he just got plain overmatched by wily pitchers executing their sequencing. He can be coaxed into expanding the zone, and there's some stiffness to the swing that leaves him vulnerable to in-zone swing-and-miss against good velocity even when he doesn't. Those tendencies are likely to get exploited more against advanced arms, and it may take some time for his game to come together at the plate.

Bret Sayre's Fantasy Take: I think we've finally gotten to the point where Petco isn't a stigma for right-handed batters anymore, but it's not the kind of park that will turn Potts into a top-10 third baseman. Good defense will keep him on the grass, but a .260 average and 20 homers just isn't what it used to be, and it doesn't even look like a top-20 option at the position in this offensive environment.

The Next Five:

11

Cal Quantrill   RHP
Born: 02/10/95   Age: 24   Bats: L   Throws: R   Height: 6'3"   Weight: 208
Origin: Round 1, 2016 Draft (#8 overall)

12. Ryan Weathers LHP
Born: 12/17/99 Age: 19 Bats: L Throws: L Height: 6'1" Weight: 200
Origin: Round 1, 2018 Draft (#7 overall)

Here we have two first-round talents—one of whom made our Top 50 last winter—and yet neither makes the Padres Top Ten. Yeah, this is a historically good system.

With Quantrill, there are some legitimate concerns with the profile now. He has an above-average fastball and a plus changeup, and the minors aren't really supposed to be a challenge for that kind of advanced arm. But his control outpaces his command at present and that was an issue for him at higher levels this year. The fastball can lack wiggle and be just a little too hittable sometimes, and the slider isn't consistent enough to keep righties off the number one. The whole can feel a little less than the sum of its parts. There's still a fair bit of the risk in the profile for an advanced college arm. Petco Park will help though, and Quantrill is likely the best pitching prospect you'll see outside of a team's Top Ten this year.

Weathers is left-handed, unlike his father David, but he did inherit the family physique. He's a shorter, stocky southpaw with a frame that we in the industry refer to as "high-maintenance." That's less of a concern when you are a potential three-pitch lefty. Weathers' fastball sits in the low-90s, but with enough armside movement to keep it off barrels. His curve flashes good 1-7 action, although the shape isn't always consistent, and it can get shorter and flatter. The change is advanced for his age, and I'm not even using it as one of my "damning with faint praise" prep change-up descriptions here. He commands all three pitches pretty well, and while he's not a huge upside play as you might expect from a top ten pick prep arm, he could certainly be Logan Allen in a couple years.

13. Josh Naylor 1B
Born: 06/22/97 Age: 22 Bats: L Throws: L Height: 5'11" Weight: 250
Origin: Round 1, 2015 Draft (#12 overall)

Naylor has long tantalized on account of an outstanding combination of bat speed, strength, and barrel control. In 2018, the 21-year-old showed signs of finally starting to consistently tap into his plus raw power, with more loft in his swing than he had previously. He managed to do that without compromising his high-end bat-to-ball ability, striking out barely more often than he took an increasingly frequent free pass.

After locking up Eric Hosmer last winter, the Padres tried to shoehorn Naylor into left field. But while he's got a sneaky little burst that belies his husky, mature frame, he lacks the agility to muster average defense at the cold corner, and the raw foot speed just isn't going to cut it on the grass. Something's going to have to give, however, as the bat increasingly looks like it can thrive against the sport's best pitchers.

14 Jacob Nix   RHP
Born: 01/09/96   Age: 23   Bats: R   Throws: R   Height: 6'4"   Weight: 220
Origin: Round 3, 2015 Draft (#86 overall)

A groin issue cost Nix the first two months of the season, but he cruised through Double-A and made one Triple-A start before getting pressed into service in the major league rotation. It went… less well. The culprit for Nix was once again his command. His fastball and curve are both above-average pitches. The fastball has some late run down in the zone, but he tends to leave it up. The curve shows good tight downer action, but he can struggle to start it in the zone. The change tends to play below-average. It's a solid fourth-starter profile, but Nix lacks the upside of the arms above him and is at risk of getting squeezed out of rotation consideration in the next season-and-a-half or so. Until then though, the Padres will need to send five dudes out there every five days, so he should get another shot or two.

15 Buddy Reed   OF
Born: 04/27/95   Age: 24   Bats: B   Throws: R   Height: 6'4"   Weight: 210
Origin: Round 2, 2016 Draft (#48 overall)

Reed is as impressive an athlete as you'll find on a baseball field, with quick-twitch movements, a flash of a first step, plus-plus straight-line speed, and tapered strength throughout his frame. The physicality has tantalized scouts for many years, and the Padres popped him in the second round despite widespread concerns about his swing and approach. After implementing a series of mechanical adjustments and dominating the Australian League last winter, Reed carried over his success through the first half, when he raked his way through High-A.

A switch hitter with prototypical swing plane differences—more length and loft from the left—his bat crashed back to Earth after a midseason promotion to Double-A, where pitchers exploited his aggressive approach and tendency to get disjointed and off-balance against off-speed pitches. His defensive ceiling—it's an easy plus glove in center with enough arm to play right—and the utility of his blazing speed will keep him on a big-league trajectory even if he never quite hits, but it's the ongoing evolution of his swing and refinement of his approach that will dictate whether he's more than a reserve outfielder at the highest level.

And Five More:

16. Tirso Ornelas, OF, Low-A Fort Wayne
Part of the talented group of teenagers assigned to Fort Wayne, Ornelas got off to a solid start before missing the final month of the season with a wrist injury. His smooth left-handed swing produces plus raw power. Ornelas has an advanced approach at the plate, and shows an ability to recognize secondaries

that many young players lack. In the outfield, he has the physical tools to be an above-average defender in a corner. There is still some work to be done on taking efficient routes, but he covers a lot of ground and his arm is more than adequate for right field. His power and defense suggest a future as a corner outfielder. As is often the case, it's just a matter of whether he hits enough for the power to play.

17. Jeisson Rosario, OF, Low-A Fort Wayne

A member of San Diego's large international signing class of 2016, Rosario was at the core of the young 2018 Tincaps team. His youth and rawness showed at times during the season and his power hasn't materialized yet. However, he's a quick-twitch athlete with plus speed. In the field he covers plenty of ground, has a strong arm, and projects to be an above-average center fielder. Rosario's swing is geared for gap-to-gap line drives. He has quick hands and knows the strike zone. The speed and defense will carry him a long way but continued development at the plate is key to reaching his potential as an everyday outfielder.

18. Esteury Ruiz, 2B, Low-A Fort Wayne

Whether it was facing more advanced pitching, a change in approach, or a combination of both, Ruiz's bat took a step back this year. Always aggressive, his strikeout rate climbed to nearly 30 percent and the bat to ball skills that had Arizona League evaluators buzzing disappeared. Ruiz's future is tied to his bat and, being limited defensively to second base, the pressure to hit is huge. There is hope for a rebound next season at Lake Elsinore. He's still very young and he has quick hands and above-average bat speed. There were also times later in the year when he showed glimpses of a more disciplined approach at the plate.

19. Gabriel Arias, SS, Low-A Fort Wayne

Another signing from the Padres' large international bonanza in 2016-17, Arias is already one of the best defensive players in the organization. Thin and athletic, he has plus range, soft hands, and lightning-quick transfers. Combine that with a strong, accurate arm and Arias has the makings of a future plus defender at the highest level. There were some early season struggles at the plate but he showed a more disciplined approach in the second half of the campaign, along with an uptick in power. Arias' premier defense up the middle suggests a future utility role with a chance to become an everyday player if the bat progresses.

20. Edward Olivares, OF, High-A Lake Elsinore

If you like high-waisted, wiry gazelles shagging fly balls in center, you're going to dig Olivares. The Venezuelan oozes physical projection, with lean strength throughout a very athletic frame. He moves well in space and closes hard into the gaps, with straight-line speed that'll push plus and play okaaaay on the bases as well. At the dish there's a nice baseline of hand-eye and directness to the point of contact, and he'll turn around some hellacious line drives along the way. The approach is highly aggressive, however, and he may never get on base enough for everything to come together.

Top Talents 25 and Under (born 4/1/93 or later):

1. Fernando Tatis, Jr.
2. Luis Urias
3. Francisco Mejia
4. MacKenzie Gore
5. Chris Paddack
6. Adrian Morejon
7. Franmil Reyes
8. Manuel Margot
9. Joey Lucchesi
10. Luis Patino

I'll be the first to admit that I did not see last season coming from Franmil Reyes, and certainly not on such a quick timeline. He deserves an enormous amount of credit for making rapid-fire adjustments to drag the full brunt of double-plus power into game action at the highest levels. Thirty-two dingers across Triple-A and the big leagues is a nice accomplishment on which to hang your (massive) hat, and best of all: He accomplished the feat while incrementally improving his approach along the way. There will be constant pressure for him to lose baseballs at a high rate, but so far, so good.

Everything about Margot's game seemed dimmer in 2018, and a couple of those frustrating, linger-y type injuries (bruised ribs in April, a sprained wrist in July) make it difficult to suss out the legitimacy of that backslide. Regardless, there was precious little evidence of improvement amid a disastrous what-actually-happened season. He produced an unholy triumvirate: A well below-average DRC+ fueled by a sub-three OBP, an atrocious success rate on the bases that barely cracked one in two over a not-small sample, and one of the worst defensive seasons by any center fielder in baseball, at least as far as FRAA was concerned. There's still plenty of time for Margot to turn things around, but after 277 big league games (and with arbitration looming next winter), it's getting late early for the former top prospect.

As our intrepid leader Brendan Gawlowski notes, if you're going to be a one-trick pony it is best to have a good trick. Lucchesi's funky delivery and weird pitch movements—a four-seamer with the finish of a two and a cambio that cuts—befuddled big-league hitters enough to rack up whiffs against more than a quarter of the hitters he faced. Sure, hitters deposited his misplaced offerings into the bleachers at an alarming rate, but he managed to minimize enough barreled contact overall to post comfortably above-average indicators in support of a two-plus WARP debut. A much thinner margin for error than most means the jury's out on how long he'll be able to keep the curtain drawn, however.

Beyond that, the bulk of San Diego's youth-oriented optimism still wanders heartland halls a couple years out from impact. Jose Castillo may have the next strongest case for back-end inclusion on this list among the remaining big-leaguers. The Very Large left-hander struck out a whole mess of dudes and looked very much the part of an actualizing high-leverage arm in his 38-odd innings. But in a system this flush with potential (very good) rotation arms, it's just too much of a stretch to shoehorn him in here.

Franchy Cordero's still a bag of obscene tools, but 36-percent whiff rates are also still disconcerting, even in times like these. Eric Lauer's junk didn't lack for utility in his first crack, but he nibbled a lot around the margins and the long-term ceiling questions remain. He commands in-zone pretty well and showed an ability to stay off of barrels with reasonable consistency. But it's tough to envision him threading the needle often enough to hold firm to a rotation spot once the wave of higher-ceilinged arms below him start crashing off Mission Beach. And in this organization, with this system, you have to err on the side of hope for a better tomorrow.

Part 3: Featured Articles

Year	League Percent Outside K Zone (Full Shift)	League Percent in K Zone (No Shift)	Difference
2015	54.1%	51.1%	3.0%
2016	53.3%	50.9%	2.4%
2017	52.6%	50.9%	1.7%
2018	52.0%	50.7%	1.3%

The hole in The Shift is fixing itself, and it's coming down really fast league wide. In my earlier work on The Shift, I suggested that until teams stopped having such a huge difference between their out-of-zone rate with and without The Shift on, there would just be too many walks for The Shift to make sense. It seems that all 30 of them have been working toward just that. I once estimated that it takes about 10 years for an idea to filter its way through baseball. At this rate, it looks like teams are going to catch up a lot faster than that. And yeah, they're all saber-smart now.

It's likely that whatever magic it was that the Rockies and Pirates had has made its way to Texas and Queens. Or is at least on its way. And if teams are committing to fixing the walk problem, then it's likely that they will continue shifting and shifting a lot.

And eventually it's going to actually make sense for them to do it.

—*Russell Carleton is a former author of Baseball Prospectus and now an analyst for the New York Mets.*

Part 3: Featured Articles

The Hole in The Shift is Fixing Itself

Russell Carleton

I've been on a bit of a mission against The Shift of late. I'm not out to get The Shift for the usual reasons that people oppose it. The words "the right way to play the game" won't be found on my lips. If a team wants to pursue a strategy that is within the rules and it works, then by all means, they have my blessing (not that they need it). Instead, my concern with The Shift is a worry that it doesn't work, or at least that it has a flaw that needs fixing.

The data show that while The Shift does a decent job of preventing singles on balls in play (what it's supposed to do), it also increases the number of walks that happen in front of it, and the number of additional walks outweighs the number of singles saved. It's a problem because you can't throw a guy out if he gets to walk to first base.

But the "why" was important. It seemed that The Shift was changing the way in which pitchers pitched. We saw that there were fewer fastballs thrown in front of The Shift than we might otherwise expect, and that pitchers tended to stay out of the strike zone a little more. Not by a lot. In fact, it might not even be visible to the naked eye. The percentage of pitches that are out of the zone goes from 51.0 to 53.3 from a standard defense (two right/two left) to a full shift (three on one side). That difference stands up even after we control for the types of hitters that get shifted against. And it's enough to drive up the walk rate to where it cancels out the benefits that teams thought they were getting with The Shift... and then some.

But there was some hope. I found that when individual pitchers stayed closer to the in-zone/out-of-zone mix that they used without The Shift on, they could still get the benefits of The Shift without the walk problems. So, in theory, a team could simply figure out a way to convince its pitchers to not fall prey to the walk trap and The Shift would once again be their friend.

It's reasonable to think that some teams might be more hip to this idea than others. Maybe some figured it out a year before the others. Maybe they were better at getting the message across to their pitchers. Or, maybe no one has figured it out yet.

Warning! Gory Mathematical Details Ahead!

I used data from 2015-2017, made available through MLB's data portal, Baseball Savant. They are kind enough to note when teams are using an infield shift (three fielders on one side of second base), as opposed to a "strategic shift" (someone's playing a bit out of position, but it's not quite that drastic) or a "standard" alignment.

Since we're doing this by team, I can't just look at raw walk rates, because we know that some teams have good pitchers and others have not-so-good pitchers. Some have a mix of both. I used the log-odds ratio method to take into account a batter's general walking proclivities, and a pitcher's as well, and then shoving them into a binary logistic regression. Then, I asked the computer to generate a specific coefficient for each team's pitchers, for when they went into The Shift and how that affected their walk rate.

Using those coefficients, I was able to project what would happen if a league-average pitcher faced a league-average hitter (which we expect would produce a league-average walk rate; from 2015-2017, 7.7 percent of plate appearances ended in a walk) and then just switched his hat. Here's the top five and the bottom five:

Top 5 Teams	Projected Shift Walk Rate	Bottom 5 Teams	Projected Shift Walk Rate
Rockies	6.2%	Rangers	11.2%
Pirates	6.7%	Mets	10.4%
Indians	7.2%	Dodgers	10.2%
Astros	7.3%	Cardinals	9.9%
Braves	7.7%	Tigers	9.7%

There are probably people out there right now trying to figure out what the common thread is among the top and bottom teams. I'm sure, because this is Baseball Prospectus, people are already trying to make the case that sabermetric "early adopters" have some sort of edge here. I think that the more interesting piece is that by the time you get to fifth place in The Shift, we're at league average.

As a sanity check, I examined the issue on a pitch-by-pitch level, looking at how often pitchers threw their pitches in the GameDay strike zone, and again using the same basic methodology and getting team-specific coefficients. The names on the list re-arranged themselves, but the idea was the same, and the two lists correlated with an R of .593.

There's a reason that I don't usually do this type of leaderboard post. I don't really know what the Rockies, Pirates, Indians, Astros, and Braves have in common, or what they have that the bottom five don't. I can put a shrug emoji here and say, "Well, it must be something!" but that seems like a cop-out. Instead, I'd like to present another table and suggest that the table above doesn't even really matter anymore.

The State of the Quality Start

Rob Mains

One of the seven things you (probably) didn't know about the 2018 season is that quality starts—defined as a start lasting six or more innings with three or fewer earned runs allowed—as a percentage of total starts cratered to an all-time low of 41 percent. I want to look a little more deeply into this, since it's been a while (May of 2016, to be exact) since I've examined quality starts.

The term *quality start* is credited to *Philadelphia Inquirer* sportswriter John Lowe. It's been derided ever since he coined it in December of 1985. Three runs in six innings? That's a 4.50 ERA! In what world is that a measure of quality?

Let's start with that criticism. It's true that 3 x 9 / 6 = 4.5. (You came here for this sort of high-level math, right?) But it's also true that type of start, meeting the bare minimum for earning a quality start, is unusual. Here's the proportion of quality starts in which the pitcher lasted exactly six innings and yielded exactly three earned runs. (I'm going to confine this analysis to the 30-team era, 1998-present. Almost all data retrieved in this article is via the Baseball-Reference Play Index.)

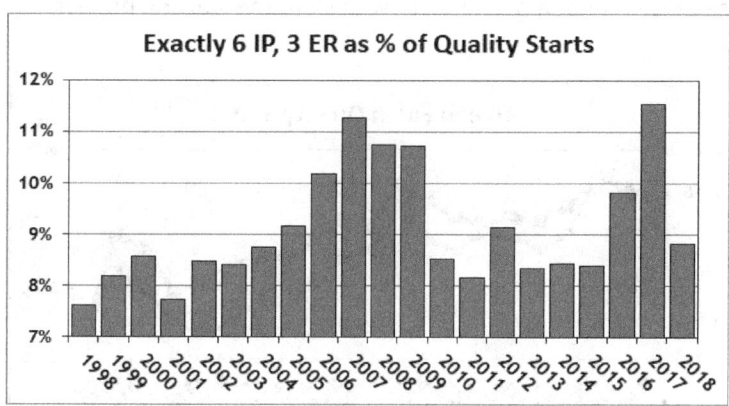

There were 1,997 quality starts in 2018. Only 176, or fewer than one in 11, featured a pitcher going six innings and allowing three earned runs. Put another way, the percentage of quality starts that resulted in a 4.50 ERA (8.8 percent) is less than half the percentage of games in which a batter hit two home runs and his team lost (22.5 percent; 237-69 won-lost). That doesn't impugn hitting two homers.

So if a 4.50 ERA isn't the norm, what is? How good are quality starts?

Pretty good, it turns out. First, on a team level:

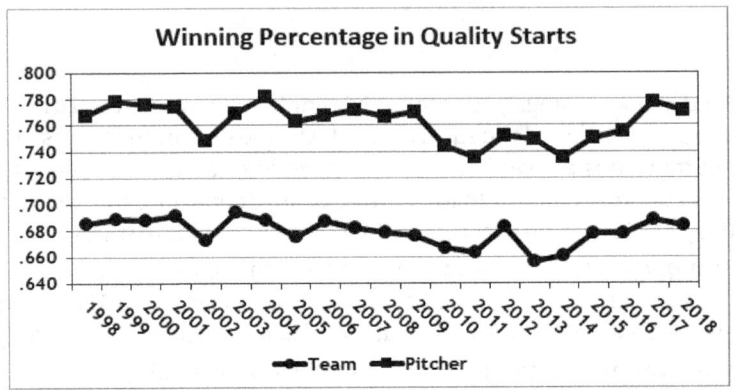

Teams receiving a quality start from their pitcher won 68.4 percent of their games in 2018, in line with the 30-team era average of 67.9 percent. A team with a .684 winning percentage wins 111 games. Getting a quality start is definitely a good thing. Individual pitchers throwing quality starts have a higher winning percentage because a big slice of team losses is assigned to a reliever.

If teams do well in quality starts, how well do the starting pitchers do? Again, very well.

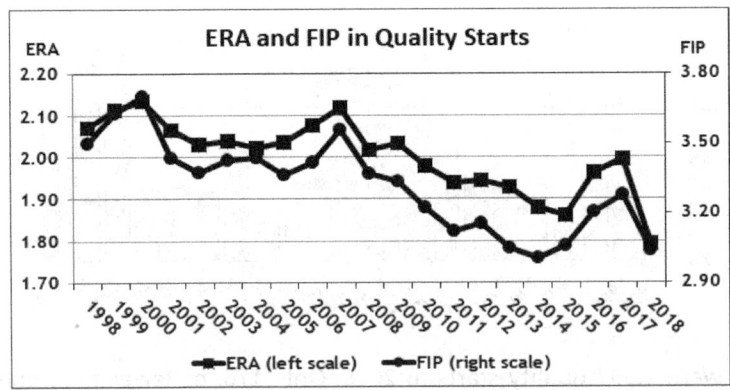

Pitchers in quality starts had a 1.79 ERA (blue line) in 2018, *the lowest in the 30-team era*. Their FIP was higher, 3.04, but still excellent. In the 30-team era, only 2014 had a lower FIP for quality starts, 3.01.

But, of course, the run environment in 2014 was different. Teams in 2014 scored 4.07 runs per game, the fewest in a non-strike year since 1976. They scored 4.45 runs per game in 2018. So surrendering a 3.04 FIP in 2018 is more impressive than 3.01 in 2014. Accordingly, let's look at ERA and FIP in quality starts relative to league averages.

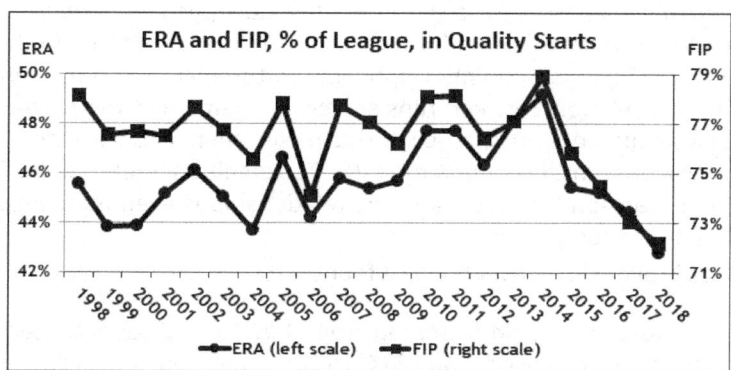

This tells a more dramatic story. Starting pitchers in 2018 gave up a 4.19 ERA and a 4.21 FIP. Starters in quality starts gave up a 1.79 ERA, 43 percent of the league average. Starters in quality starts gave up a 3.04 FIP, 72 percent of the league average. Both of these marks represent lows in the 30-team era.

The takeaway here is this: *Quality starts are better, relative to other starts, than they've ever been over the past 21 years.*

Maybe during the winter I'll look at this over a longer arc of time. For now, though, we can definitively say quality starts are the best they've ever been since the Diamondbacks and Rays joined the majors.

Yet, paradoxically, they're down.

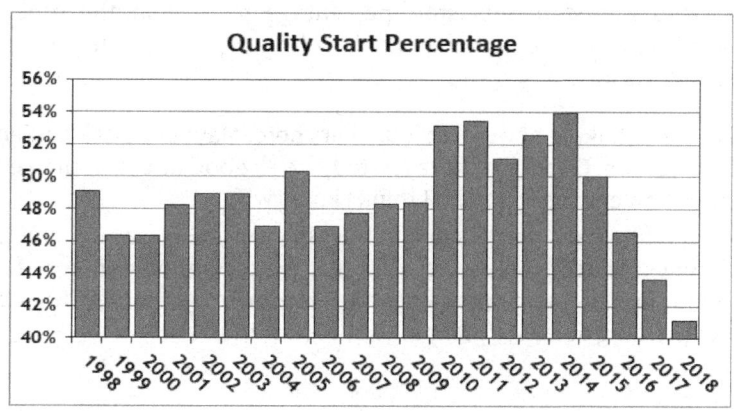

Heads-Up Hacking—The First Pitch

Matthew Trueblood

Batters fell behind in a higher percentage of all plate appearances in 2018 than in any previous season for which we have pitch-by-pitch data. That kind of granular information goes back only to 1988, but we might safely assume (given all we know about baseball as it had been before that, and as it has been in the years since) that batters have *never* fallen behind at a higher rate than they did last season.

Through the 1990s, the percentage of all plate appearances that began 0-1 hovered in the high 30s and low 40s. In the 2000s, it rose steadily but slowly, through the mid-40s. In 2018, 49.8 percent of all trips to the plate began 0-1. That, as much as anything, captures in microcosm the nature of hitting in MLB today.

A countdown clock toward strike three begins ticking almost the moment a batter takes his place in the box. The league's adjusted OPS+ on the first pitch was higher in 2018 than ever before, and that has been true in most of the last 10 seasons. Batters hit .264/.289/.442 in all plate appearances in which they swung at the first pitch last season, and .241/.330/.395 in all plate appearances in which they took that first offering.

The percentage differences in batting average and isolated power there favor swinging at the first pitch by more than in any season since 1988, while the difference in on-base percentage favors taking by more than ever. If you want to get on base at a decent clip, it's a good idea to be patient, but you run the risk of missing the only chances you'll get to produce power.

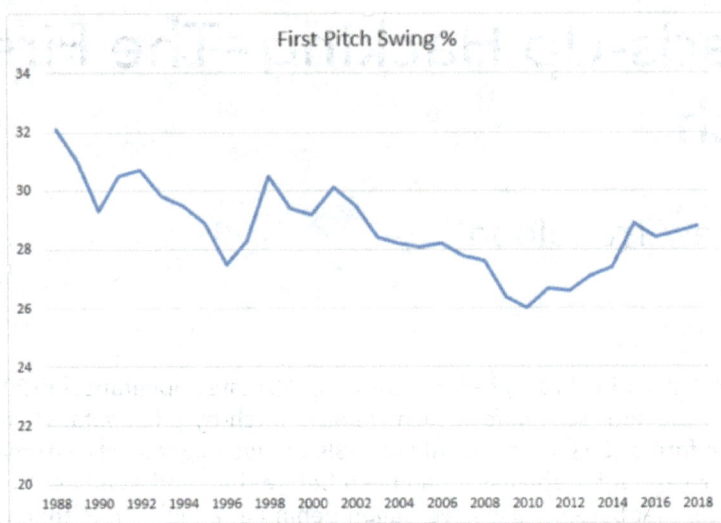

The league swung at the first pitch 28.8 percent of the time in 2018. With the isolated exception of 2015, that's the highest that number has climbed since 2002, but it might not be high enough. With the help of BP research maven Rob McQuown, I looked at the aggregate Called Strike Probability (CSProb) on the first pitch for each season since 2008, when the implementation of PITCHf/x first made measuring that possible. It's risen sharply during that period.

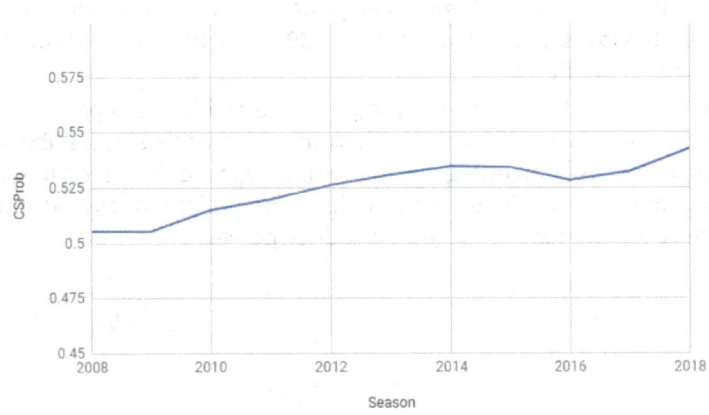

Called Strike Probability, First Pitch of PA (2008-2018)

Instead, it's sitting at a low ebb, and while it does so, even guys who get on base often are a little less helpful than they were 10 years ago—or 20, or 40, or 60, or 70, or 80, or 90. They're less helpful, that is, because unless there happen to be three or four other guys in the lineup who get on just as regularly, their contribution is merely to forestall the inevitable. Runs happen, increasingly, when a sudden bang happens, and that means attacking early in the count—because pitchers are sure as hell doing that.

In a league making contact on barely 75 percent of its swings, and a league in which an increasing number of pitchers can throw multiple off-speed pitches for strikes in any count, the only way to consistently generate offense is going to be aggressive. This isn't necessarily true for individuals, like Mookie Betts and Jose Ramirez, who make a lot of contact and have excellent plate discipline, and whose power comes from such natural quickness in a short stroke. Most players have to make tradeoffs, though, whether it be lowering their contact rate or raising their chase rate, in order to consistently make the quality of contact necessary to survive in today's game.

Highest %	Lowest %
Javier Baez – 48.3	Joe Mauer – 4.6
Freddie Freeman – 47.1	Mookie Betts – 9.7
Ozzie Albies – 46.3	Brett Gardner – 10.7
Jose Altuve – 44.2	Jose Ramirez – 12.0
Nick Castellanos – 44.1	Jason Kipnis – 13.8
Joey Gallo – 42.3	Jesus Aguilar – 14.5
Corey Dickerson – 40.9	Xander Bogaerts – 15.8
Salvador Perez – 40.8	Brian Dozier – 16.3
Eddie Rosario – 40.7	Mike Trout – 17.6
Nick Ahmed – 40.4	Yasmani Grandal – 17.6

Top 10 and Bottom 10 Hitters, First-Pitch Swing Rate (2018)

The question isn't which of these lists one prefers, but what they each convey, qualitatively, about the cat-and-mouse game of early-count hitting. Those top five on the left, especially, drive home the fact that for most players, getting aggressive early in the count is now key to keeping strikeout rate down and hitting for power.

For now, the message is: pitchers are coming right after batters with the nastiest stuff they've ever had. Batters had better stop giving away strike one and force hurlers to adjust, or the global OBP crisis is only going to get worse.

—*Matthew Trueblood is an author of Baseball Prospectus.*

A Hymn for the Index Stat

Patrick Dubuque

We survived without computers. I know this, because I remember the day when my dad hooked up his brand-new Atari 400 computer to the back of our 12-inch Magnavox television, and the perfect blue of the memo pad lit up for the first time. I was born just on the edge of that transitional generation, of learning cursive and balancing checkbooks and just doing math all the time, constant manual arithmetic.

It still amazes me. We learned how to sail ships without computers. We learned how to do calculus. We built towers that didn't fall down, most of the time. We engineered catapults to knock them down anyway. We built a robust system of philosophy called "utilitarianism," founded on the principle that the good of an action is evaluated by summing the effects of that action, which is the kind of formula that would make the world's mainframes crash. The whole foundation of statistics as a field is "here's math you could easily do but would die of old age first."

The fact of the matter is that there is too much math in the world to do. There are too many things changing, and too many things too small to notice, for us to handle. At some point, they become too much for the computers to handle as well, which is why we have chaos theory and undetectable earthquakes, but it's not an even fight. At some point, we fall back on intuition, and given how under-equipped we are, we're forced to bestow that intuition with some sort of supernatural superiority, the "gut feeling," that we can't prove because we can only intuit that our intuition is better.

We're all lousy at intuition, and wonderful at lying to ourselves about it. The honest truth is that computers are far better at intuition than we are, because in order to know what feels "off" you have to know what's "on." In order to do that you have to constantly reassess the average of everything, then re-rank your own experience against it.

Test your own, by comparing these three anonymous lines:

Player	G	HR	AVG	OBP	SLG
Player A	156	38	.259	.342	.535
Player B	154	38	.280	.348	.527
Player C	158	38	.266	.343	.509

Index of Names

Allen, Austin 99
Allen, Logan 90, 108
Arias, Gabriel 99
Baez, Michel 91, 109
Campusano, Luis 99
Castillo, Jose 45
Cordero, Franchy 20
Cordoba, Allen 99
Craig, Allen 99
Diaz, Miguel 47
Edwards, Xavier 81
Erlin, Robbie 49
Espinoza, Anderson 92
France, Ty 99
Garcia, Greg 99
Gore, MacKenzie 93, 106
Guerra, Javier 99
Hedges, Austin 22
Hosmer, Eric 24
Jankowski, Travis 26
Kennedy, Brett 51
Kinsler, Ian 28
Lauer, Eric 53
Lawson, Reggie 100
Loup, Aaron 55
Lucchesi, Joey 57
Machado, Manny 30
Makita, Kazuhisa 100
Margot, Manuel 32
Maton, Phil 59
Mejia, Francisco 34, 105
Mitchell, Bryan 61
Morejon, Adrian 94, 107
Munoz, Andres 100
Myers, Wil 37
Naylor, Josh 82, 111
Nix, Jacob 63, 112
Olivares, Edward 99, 113
Ornelas, Tirso 99, 112
Paddack, Chris 95, 106
Patino, Luis 96, 107
Perdomo, Luis 65
Pirela, Jose 39
Potts, Hudson 83, 110
Powell, Boog 84
Quantrill, Cal 97, 110
Reed, Buddy 85, 112
Renfroe, Hunter 41
Reyes, Franmil 43
Richards, Garrett 67
Rosario, Jeisson 99, 113
Ruiz, Esteury 86, 113
Solis, Sammy 100
Stammen, Craig 69
Stewart, Chris 87
Stock, Robert 71
Strahm, Matt 73
Tatis Jr., Fernando 88, 103
Torrens, Luis 99
Urias, Luis 89, 104
Warren, Adam 75
Weathers, Ryan 98, 111

San Diego Padres 2019

Wieck, Brad 100
Wingenter, Trey 77
Yates, Kirby 79

This graph covers only the 30-team era. In my article last week, though, I looked at the years 1908-2018. The result was the same. The 41 percent of starts in 2018 that were quality starts are an all-time low, well below the runners-up: 1930's 43 percent (the year teams scored an all-time record 5.55 runs per game) and last year's 44 percent.

The normal explanation for a dip in quality start percentage is an increase in scoring. When teams score a lot of runs, it's harder for starting pitchers to last six or more innings and limit opponents to three earned runs. From 1998 to 2014, the correlation between runs scored per game and the percentage of starts that were quality starts was -0.94. That means there was an extremely close relationship: More runs, fewer quality starts. Too small a sample? Go back to the start of the Expansion Era, 1961, and the relationship is even more negative, a -0.95 correlation, though 2014.

But that's broken down over the past four years:

- 2015: Runs per game increased from 4.07 to 4.25, quality start percentage decreased from 54.0 to 50.1. Yes, that's a negative relationship, but the regression model would predict a decline of 1.5 percentage points. We got 3.9 instead.
- 2016: Runs per game increased from 4.25 to 4.48, quality start percentage decreased from 50.1 to 46.6. Past experience would suggest a decline of just 1.8 percentage points. We got 3.4.
- 2017: Runs per game increased from 4.48 to 4.65, quality start percentage decreased from 46.6 to 43.6. Again, the direction's right, but the magnitude isn't. Using the relationship from 1998 to 2014, that increase in scoring should've reduced quality starts by 1.3 percentage points, not 2.9.
- 2018: Runs per game declined from 4.65 to 4.45. That should've resulted in the quality start percentage moving in the other direction, rising 1.6 points. It didn't. It fell 2.6 points, as noted, to an all-time low.

Granted, we're talking about just four years here. Maybe they're outliers. But I don't think they are. Quality starts, as noted, are as good or better than ever. But they're rarer than ever as well. And I think I know why.

To get a quality start, you need to allow three or fewer earned and pitch at least six innings. That's 18 outs. Here's a graph showing the number of starting pitchers who limited their opponents to three or fewer earned runs but got pulled after pitching at least five innings but fewer than six:

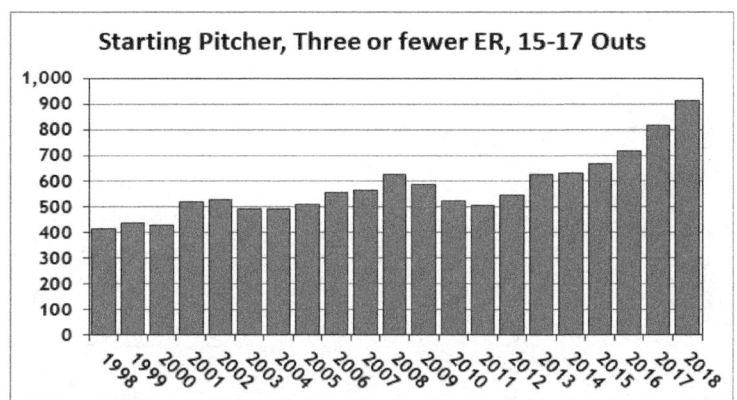

A pitcher getting 15 outs pitched five innings. A pitcher getting 16 outs pitched 5 1/3. A pitcher getting 17 outs pitched 5 2/3. More than ever before, pitchers are being removed from games in which they are within 1-3 outs of a quality start, falling just short of the six-inning finish line. Widespread acknowledgement of the times-through-the-order penalty and a flotilla of available bullpen arms is making the quality start simultaneously both more excellent and more rare.

Which is ironic, given that we saw a new post-war quality start record this season:

Rank	Pitcher	Season	Consecutive QS
1	Jacob deGrom	2018	24
2	Bob Gibson	1968	22
-	Chris Carpenter	2005	22
4	Johan Santana	2004	21
5	Luis Tiant	1968	20
-	Mike Scott	1986	20
-	Jake Arrieta	2015	20
8	Robin Roberts	1952	19
-	Tom Seaver	1973	19
-	Jack Morris	1983	19
-	Greg Maddux	1998	19
-	Josh Johnson	2010	19
-	Jon Lester	2014	19

While there have been longer streaks spread over multiple seasons, no pitcher since World War II threw more consecutive quality starts in one year than Jacob deGrom this year. The fact that he did in a year in which quality starts were the rarest they've ever been adds to the accomplishment.

—*Rob Mains is an author of Baseball Prospectus.*

Called Strike Probability is exactly what it sounds like: a pitch with a given CSProb has roughly that chance of being called a strike, if not swung at. In 2018, a batter who took 100 first pitches from a random sampling of the league's pitchers might expect to fall behind 54 or 55 times—up from 50 or 51 times in 2008. Almost regardless of pitch type (and, notably, especially in the case of fastballs), the first pitch tends to have more of the zone right now than ever before.

Pitchers are better at throwing strikes. They have better stuff, and believe more in their ability to miss bats within the zone. Perhaps most importantly, they know that batters are looking for one thing on the first pitch: a fastball. If they don't get it, they're likely to take the pitch. Check out how the use of sinkers and four-seamers on the first pitch has changed in a decade:

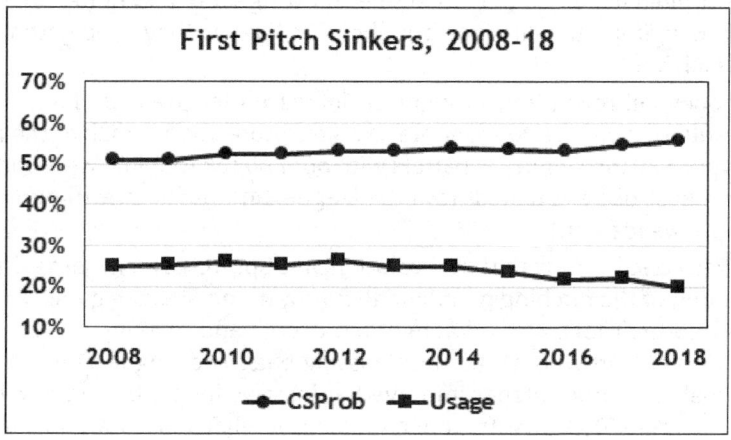

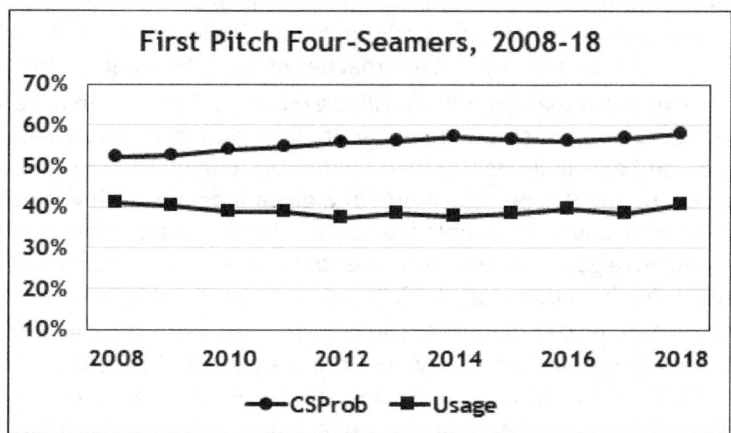

The sinker is losing its place in baseball, but the rate at which pitchers have thrown it on the first pitch hasn't dropped any faster than its usage rate in other counts. Pitchers have actually gone to their four-seamer *more* often to open counts, in the last few years, after a dip in the 2012-2015 period. What's really changed, though, and what shows up in both charts above, is that pitchers are catching more of the zone with first-pitch fastballs than they were a decade ago, or a half-decade ago. They're attacking right away, even with the pitch they know batters are expecting. The message is pretty clear: batters are being too passive.

Sliders, curves, and changeups each have more of the zone when thrown on the first pitch than they did several years ago, too, though the effect is less pronounced. Pitchers have seen the numbers; they know batters are doing better on the first pitch itself. They still feel safe throwing more and better strikes than ever before, figuring they'll come out ahead as long as they keep getting ahead to open each battle.

The Moneyball revolution brought an increased league-wide focus on OBP, which resulted in a de facto mandate to take a more patient tack at the plate. It worked very well for a while, as batters with poor plate discipline were compelled to either adjust or be expelled from the league, and pitchers with poor control were slowly weeded out.

However, concurrent with that revolution, and spurred by it in some ways, was the evolution of the pitching paradigm that now dominates the game. As batters ratcheted up their focus on inflating pitch counts and working walks, pitchers honed theirs on throwing strikes and missing bats. The league's understanding of what makes a good pitcher improved at least as much, from the mid-1990s through the mid-2000s, as its understanding of what makes a good hitter. As amphetamines and other performance-enhancing drugs were phased mostly out of the game, and as PITCHf/x broke onto the scene, individuals and teams learned how to exploit the evolved approaches of even the smartest hitters.

The ability to avoid making outs is still the most valuable one in baseball, but the magnitude of its eclipse of slugging is smaller than ever. To a greater extent than power, on-base skills derive their value from chaining—from the on-base skill levels of the players on either side of a given individual. Eleven years ago, when the housing crisis hit, people learned the hard way that the value of their homes depended a good deal on the values of their neighbors' homes. The same wasn't true, though, of their cars. So it is now, with OBP and SLG.

The global OBP in 2018 was .318. The only seasons since the Dead Ball Era in which the league got on base at a worse clip were 2013-2015, 1988, 1971-1972, and 1963-1968. This is all happening despite the aforementioned evolution of the science of hitting. It's happening despite a shift in approach and focus, one that would steer OBP ever higher, if only it were working.

San Diego Padres 2019

These all seem like pretty similar players, right? The second one a touch more batted-ball dependent, the third a little less strong, but all pretty good hitters. And you'd be right, about the latter. Not the former.

Here's the breakdown:

- Player A: 1991 Howard Johnson, 141 DRC+
- Player B: 1996 Dean Palmer, 121 DRC+
- Player C: 2018 Giancarlo Stanton, 114 DRC+

Baseball is fortunate to have escaped the seismic shifts of so many other sports, where the talents and performances of other eras are nearly unrecognizable. (And not just other sports: try to explain the greatness of the movie Duck Soup without adjusting for era.) But they're still there, and they're nearly impossible to account for manually, without having to resort to sweeping generalizations like "steroid era" or juiced-ball era" to throw out entire swathes of production.

This is all to say that we should celebrate the index stat, that simple 100-based scale with such a humble aim: just to give context. It's hard to imagine how we lived without them for so long. Sabermetricians have always tried to make their stats look like other stats: True Average mapped to batting average, FIP molded to look like and compare to ERA. It's easy to understand the motivation—these statistics carry an emotional value in them that is hard to resist, as with the .300 hitter and the 2.00 ERA—but even they fall prey to the same loss of scale as their unadjusted counterparts. If a .300 average means different things in different years, does that hold true for a .300 True Average?

Instead, 100 doesn't say anything, except above average or below. And it does it instantly, for every season in every run environment for any statistic we want it to. We should have more index stats: K%+, so we can stop comparing Mike Clevinger's career 9.46 K/9 to Nolan Ryan's 9.55. HBP%+, so we can note that Ron Hunt was getting plunked when nobody else was getting plunked, as opposed to that imitator Brandon Guyer. Some might note how stale these references are and accuse league-adjustment as a backward-looking drive, and this is true. But we're always looking backward, always comparing the new with the expectations already set. The index stat just forces us to be honest.

There's always resistance to a new statistic, especially one so outwardly simple and so internally complex. We tend to stick with what we know, even in the case of formulas that are supposed to tell us what we know. But if your resistance is that it seems too complicated, too counterintuitive, too "black boxy," I encourage you to consider why you feel that way. Because the real world is infinitely more complicated than baseball, where all the pitches go in one basic direction and the baserunners are only allowed to travel in four directions. Baseball statistics based on mixed methodology are almost impossibly intricate. So are skyscrapers and automobiles. That's why we have computers—to take the guesswork out of them.

—*Patrick Dubuque is an author of Baseball Prospectus.*

Ballpark diagrams for Baseball Prospectus are created by THIRTY81Project, a design concept offering original ballpark artwork, including the new 'Ballparks of 2019' 11 x 17 color print.

Visit **www.thirty81project.com** for full details.

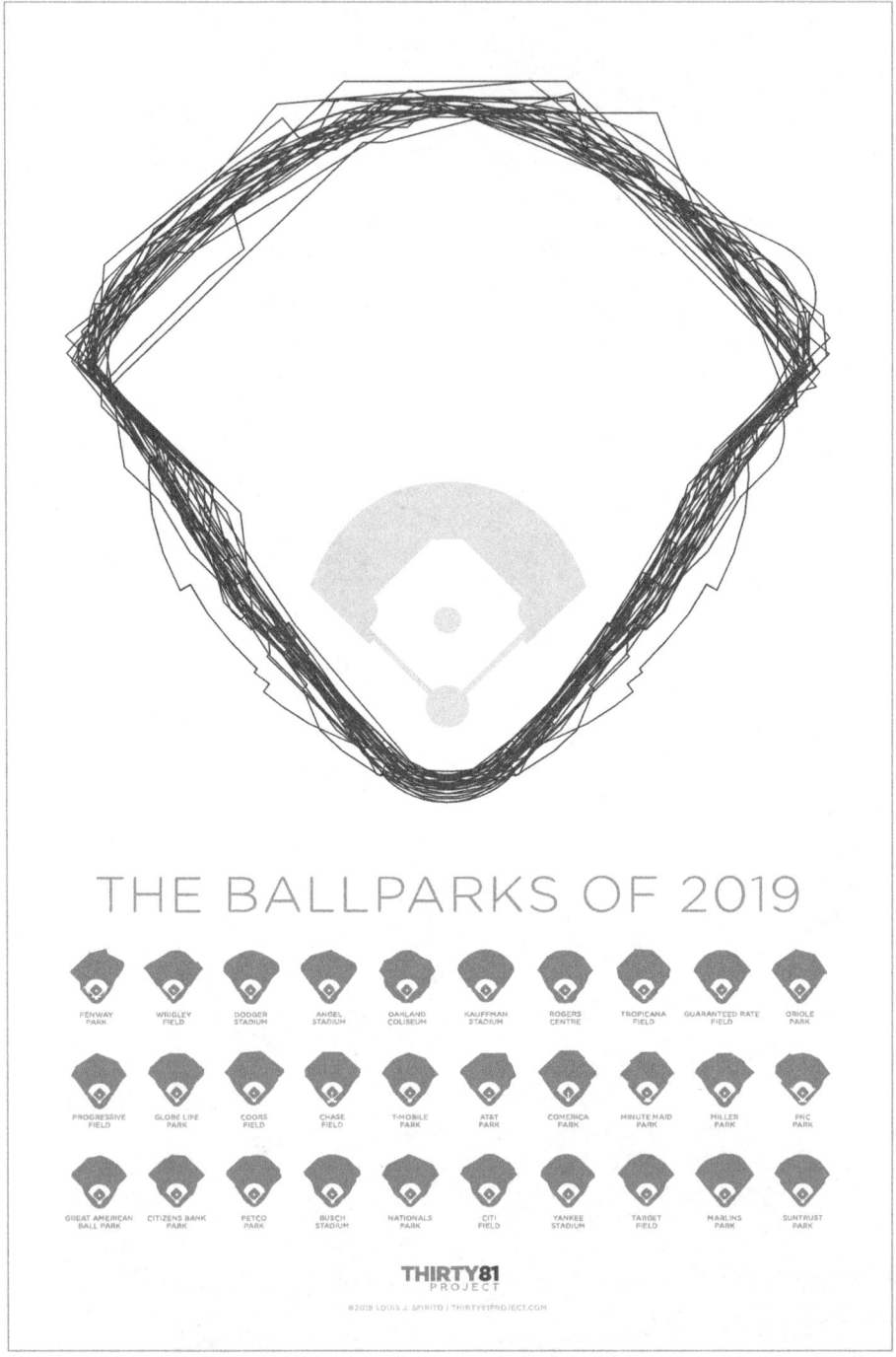